KIWIANA

KIWIANA
UNIQUELY NEW ZEALAND

Stephen Barnett & Richard Wolfe

pb potton & burton

First published in 2017 by Potton & Burton

Potton & Burton
98 Vickerman Street, PO Box 5128, Nelson, New Zealand
pottonandburton.co.nz

Text © Stephen Barnett & Richard Wolfe
Illustrations © as per pp95-96

Kiwiana is a revised edition of *New Zealand! New Zealand! – In Praise of Kiwiana*, first published 1989

ISBN 978 0 947503 51 2

Printed in China by Midas Printing International Ltd

Contents

Kia Ora

This book is a celebration of Kiwiana - a name for New Zealand's popular culture - which gathers together many of the threads that go to characterise life in these islands and which make up what is the unique New Zealand difference.

It's a quirky list covering objects, images, language and ways of doing things that typify life in this land, and to a large degree stem from the country's isolation in colonial times and the independence and self-reliance of its people. The early settlers, both Polynesian and Pākehā, had only what they brought with them; anything else they had to make or invent.

Kiwiana had its greatest consolidation over the two decades following the Second World War as the baby-boomer generation, buoyed up on a cradle-to-grave welfare state, met rising prosperity. For the average New Zealand couple and their 2.6 children it was a life of Plunket, Buzzy Bee, Saturday rugby, a beer or two, a rotary clothesline and the occasional pav. It was also a time when New Zealand began to make its mark internationally in new and different ways - when we were, for example, first to stand at the summit of the world's tallest mountain, when our

sports people were increasingly to the fore, and when we protested injustices - all of which added to the sum of what it meant to be a Kiwi.

Today this shared popular culture continues to do a good job of explaining something of life in New Zealand and its 4.7 million people, 32 million sheep (and who knows how many possums out there in the bush) and Ten Guitars.

Haere Mai and God Defend
All Blacks, baches and beaut
Silver fern, sheep and Anzacs
Swanndris, gumboots, mates
Southern Cross, She'll be right.

– Stephen Barnett and Richard Wolfe

The New Zealanders

Inhabiting a narrow stretch of ground that looks like a smallish comma on the page that is the broad Pacific Ocean, New Zealanders have, like their country's fauna and flora, been shaped by geographical isolation.

The first people to arrive in Aotearoa New Zealand came from east Polynesia in double-hulled canoes, probably around 1250AD. These early settlers found a climate and natural environment very different to that in their previous Pacific homeland, and their adaptation to the local conditions led to the distinctive culture of the Māori. The next major wave of immigration was in the mid-nineteenth century when large numbers of people began arriving from Europe. In time this influx resulted in a strong heritage of European culture and institutions, some originating here, some borrowed and adapted from elsewhere.

The 'tyranny of distance' (a term coined by Australian

The coiling koru motif was characteristic of Māori facial tattooing (moko), as seen in this c.1773 engraving The Head of a Chief of New Zealand, *based on a 1769 painting by Sydney Parkinson.*

historian Geoffrey Blainey) was at the same time a spur to the colonial making-do-with-what-you've-got mentality, and to innovation. While native ingenuity is not unique to New Zealand – other countries have their Rube Goldbergs and their Heath Robinsons – the difference here is the degree to which the No. 8 wire factor permeated society. Further back, the land's earliest settlers had also excelled in adaptation and innovation. Using only stone tools, for example, the ancestors of Māori had developed a distinctive wood-carving style, while also producing intricate carvings in stone and bone.

Māori art was in complete contrast to the European tradition, and at first was admired primarily for ethnographic reasons. However, in the second half of the nineteenth century there was growing recognition of these objects as works of art. Owen Jones, author of the standard reference book *The Grammar of Ornament* (1856), noted that Pacific objects were likely to be spared the 'superfluous ornament' frequently found on those made by European craftsmen: of a carved Māori paddle he said, 'there is not a line upon its surface misapplied.'

ABOVE *Māori art utilises forms derived from nature. The best known of these forms is the koru, as found on kōwhaiwhai (rafter patterns in meeting houses).*

RIGHT *... a distinctive carving style; such as here in the carved maihi (barge board), and amo (vertical post) of a meeting house.*

OPPOSITE *The heitiki, based on a highly stylised human figure, was usually of greenstone (pounamu).*

Māori art utilises curvilinear and organic forms, derived from nature. The best known of these forms is the koru, commonly found in Māori carving design and on kōwhaiwhai (rafter patterns in meeting houses). Based on the unfolding frond of New Zealand's silver fern (ponga), the spiralling koru is seen as symbolising rejuvenation and new life. The koru is also used in facial tattooing (moko), a process traditionally restricted to persons of rank and carried out with chisels made from shark teeth, or sharpened

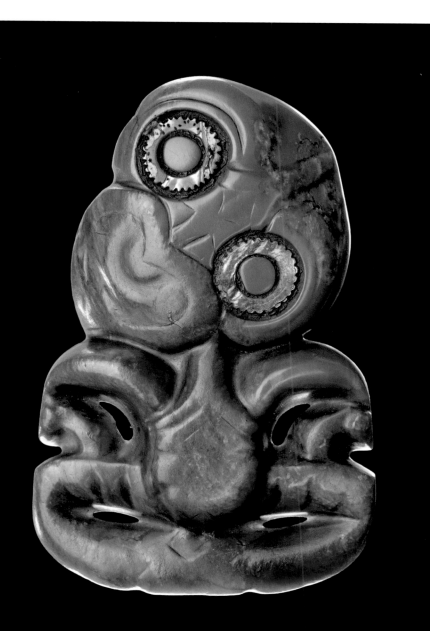

*With some No. 8 wire and a bit of lateral thinking
there wasn't much that couldn't be made, or fixed.*

bone or stone, and inks of natural pigments. Perhaps the best known example of Māori art is the heitiki, a small carved ornament based on a highly stylised human figure, usually of greenstone (pounamu) and worn around the neck.

When the organised settlement of New Zealand by Europeans began in the mid-1800s, it attracted hardy pioneers who sailed to an uncertain future on the other side of the world. What they were unable to take with them they had to go without, or improvise. This was especially so in the case of farmers in the back-blocks who had to make do with resources at hand.

One of the handiest of materials proved to be standard fencing wire, No. 8 gauge (4 mm diameter), thousands of kilometres of which would eventually encircle the farms and paddocks of New Zealand. It was frequently used in conjunction with other materials also found lying around the farm, such as pieces of 4×2 timber or empty tins. For example, a bucket could be fashioned from an empty petrol or kerosene tin using a handle formed from No. 8 wire. With this approach there wasn't much a lateral-thinking farmer couldn't make or mend, and No. 8 wire came to represent our local inventiveness.

In the 1930s a handy publication for farmers explained how an empty 44-gallon oil or fuel drum could be converted into a wheelbarrow, water cart or a tray for feeding sheep. But perhaps the most creative of the four hundred or so suggested ideas was a mouse trap made by smearing a baking powder tin (probably an Edmonds tin) with butter and setting it to spin on a shaft at the top of an empty kerosene tin. The hapless mouse jumped on to the buttered baking powder tin, only to lose its foothold and end up trapped at the bottom of the kerosene tin.

A more extraordinary expression of back-block innovation was that of Temuka farmer Richard Pearse, who in 1906 was a granted a patent for a flying machine on which appeared the first known ailerons (moveable wing-flaps). One of Pearse's flying machines may also have made the world's first powered (if not wholly controlled) flight in 1903, taking off before the Wright Brothers. This was achieved by a man who had no formal training, built the motors by himself and taught himself to fly reading magazine articles.

Similarly ground-breaking New Zealand inventions and innovations in the years since include the Hamilton jet boat, the Gallagher electric fence and the development of aerial topdressing, this country being the first to successfully distribute seeds and fertiliser by means of light aircraft. This ability to apply lateral thinking to realise an idea's potential, along with determination and perseverance to see it into realisation, is a regular feature of our history.

The influx of settlers from Europe into New Zealand in the years following 1840 had a huge impact on the life of Māori. Not least was the introduction of communicable diseases that resulted in a dramatic decline in the Māori population, which reached its lowest point in the 1890s. For the larger part of the twentieth century Māori lived at the margins, and it was not until the 1950s that the beginnings of major changes within Māori society were seen. Māori were now moving from rural areas to the towns and cities and enjoying an increasing profile that resulted in a growing awareness of the country's biculturalism. In 1975 the New Zealand government established a tribunal to investigate breaches of the country's founding document, the Treaty of Waitangi. In particular, this recognised the growing concern at the dispossession of Māori land, and the tribunal began to consider claims and the need to make reparations for past confiscations. The Treaty now became a focus of Māori protest; there were calls for equal partnership and the reassertion of Māori identity. A highly publicised land march, or hīkoi, a 640-kilometre walk from Te Hāpua in the Far North to Wellington, protested at the loss of Māori land. Three years later, in 1978, similar concerns also provoked a protest at Raglan, in Waikato, over Māori land that had been requisitioned during the Second World War for an airfield that was never built. In 1977 Ngāti Whātua people of Ōrākei, Auckland, began an occupation of Bastion Point. This was in reaction to the government announcement of a housing development on a former Ngāti Whātua reserve that had been gradually reduced by compulsory acquisition. The stand-off ended 506 days later, when police and army personnel removed 222 protesters, and following a Waitangi Tribunal inquiry in the mid-1980s, much of the contested land was later returned to its original owners.

An important feature of the renaissance of Māori indigenous culture was the drive to preserve the Māori language. In 1840, the year of the signing of the Treaty, the predominant language in Aotearoa

New Zealand was built on hard work and on the basis of equal opportunity and a fair go. CLOCKWISE FROM TOP LEFT Woman in milking shed, high-country shepherd, men digging tunnel, meatworks, sawyers with log, coalminers boarding a bus.

New Zealand was of course Māori. But within three decades, government policy required that only the English language was to be used in the education of Māori children. A century on, growing concerns led to a Māori Language Petition being presented to Parliament in 1972. This resulted in the 1987 Māori Language Commission, established to promote the Māori language – te reo Māori – as a living language, and as an official language of New Zealand.

New Zealand has been hugely fortunate to enjoy a mix of cultures – Māori and European, and more recently that of Pacific and Asian peoples – that has contributed much to the making of the New Zealand character – which is in large measure friendly and open-handed – and to the making of a society which was until recent years highly regarded for its egalitarianism and sense of fair play. It was in New Zealand that the 40-hour week was established, the idea of Samuel Parnell, a British immigrant of 1840 who reasoned that a person's labour should be just eight hours and no more (based on the idea of eight hours work, eight hours sleep, eight hours for oneself). In response to one employer's retort that 'in London workers arrive on the job by 6 a.m. or have their pay docked', Parnell's reply was 'we're not in London'.

Prime Minister Richard Seddon, writing in his party's manifesto of 1904, acknowledged that the 'spirit of self-respecting independence already marks our people and I would have the title "New Zealander" imply, the world over, a type of manhood, strenuous, independent and humane'.

Such qualities were expressed, not least, in the acronym ANZAC that was given to those in the New Zealand defence forces in the two world wars in tandem with their Australian cousins. 'ANZAC' was the telegraph address for the Australian and New Zealand Army Corps stationed in Egypt during the First World War, and the action of those first ANZACs on Turkey's Gallipoli Peninsula was to sear the name into the minds of both countries for ever after.

A disastrous British military strategy had thrown the ANZACs on to a small curve of beach under steep cliffs (the place known then as Gaba Tepe, now as Anzac Cove), where they were expected, against heavy odds, not only to knock out Turkish positions on the high ground inland, but also to then cross the Peninsula and immobilise Turkish forts on the Dardenelle Straits. In the first three days of the April 1915 landings 900 Kiwis were killed. Eight months later, when the remnants of the ANZAC force were evacuated, the total was 2700 New Zealanders dead and many thousands more wounded.

ABOVE *The action New Zealand forces saw on Turkey's Gallipoli Peninsula in the First World War meant we would for ever after remember the name ANZAC.*
OPPOSITE *Sir Edmund Hillary, the first to climb Mt Everest, typified 'a type of manhood, strenuous, independent and humane'.*

An Essential Kiwiana

In the 1940s New Zealand writer John Mulgan identified the preoccupations of his fellow countrymen: 'Our main pursuits were only cultural in the broadest sense. They were horse-racing, playing Rugby football, and beer-drinking – especially playing football.' He acknowledged that there were other 'minor' activities, such as yachting and mountaineering, but rugby was the main one, being 'religion and desire and fulfilment all in one'. These interests of the stereotypical Kiwi were celebrated in the mid-1960s in the song 'Rugby, Racing and Beer' by Christchurch-born Rod Derrett, whose distinctive brand of local humour was also apparent in such other compositions as 'Puha and Pakeha', 'The Kiwi Train' and '6 O'clock Swill'.

New Zealand's national game had its origins in England in the 1820s. It first kicked off in this country in Nelson, in 1870, and in July of the following year a group of enthusiasts also tried it out on a paddock in Wellington. Although at that stage few were familiar with the rules, before long rugby was said to be 'all the rage' and spreading throughout the country. Interprovincial matches began in 1875 and our first national team played overseas, in New South Wales, in 1884. The New Zealand Rugby Football Union was formed in 1892, and the following year it adopted the now famous black jersey. It was in 1905 when the national team was touring Britain for the first time that it began to be known as the 'All Blacks'; as such the team has gone on to dominate world rugby ever since.

As for the second activity on Mulgan's list, horse-racing, race meetings soon became important social and sporting events in the country's new colonial settlements. Clubs were formed, one of the earliest and most durable being the Canterbury Jockey Club, which held its first meeting in 1855. Racecourses and their wooden grandstands became local landmarks – today there are still about 50 throughout the country, from Ruakaka, near Whangarei, in the north, to Invercargill's Ascot Park in the south – and betting on horses became New Zealand's most popular form of gambling. This led to the automatic totalisator (the 'tote') being invented by George Julius, who lived in this country in the 1890s, with the first such machine installed at Auckland's Ellerslie racecourse in 1913.

In 1951 the TAB – the Totalisator Agency Board – became the sole betting operator in New Zealand. Horse-racing dominated local gambling for decades afterwards until the 1980s, when alternatives such as gaming machines, casinos and lotteries were introduced, along with betting on other sports like rugby and cricket.

Both rugby and racing were beaten to New Zealand by beer however, first introduced by Captain Cook in March 1773. Using the leaves of rimu and other native trees, he produced a brew designed to combat scurvy among his crew. No doubt a much more refreshing drop was produced by the country's first commercial brewery, established in 1835 by Joel Polack in Kororāreka (now Russell), in the Bay of Islands. Like rugby and racing clubs, breweries were soon springing up everywhere, and by the turn of the twentieth century there were about a hundred throughout the country.

In 1918, as a result of war restrictions and pressure from the temperance movement, the nation's pubs were forced to close at 6 p.m. This resulted in an uncivilised hour of binge drinking after knocking off work at 5, the infamous '6 o'clock swill', which lasted until 1967 when the country voted for change: pubs could now stay open until 10 p.m. By now the market was dominated by just two companies, Lion and Dominion Breweries, offering a limited choice of mass-produced beers. Today's drinker is more discerning, and in recent years there has been an explosion in the growth of the craft-beer business. By August 2017 the country had 194 craft breweries, producing more than 1600 unique beers, among them such locally flavoured names as Aotearoa, Kereru, Moa and Tuatara.

There's a lot more to the nation's main pursuits today than rugby, racing and beer, but these activities remain stalwarts of popular culture alongside the likes of bungy jumping, marching girls, Edmonds 'Sure to Rise', gumboots, Buzzy Bees, L&P, sheep, hokey-pokey ice cream and pavlova, and we shouldn't forget the influence on our popular culture of a uniquely Kiwi slang that can be both colourful and droll and which mixes European and Māori contributions. There are constant new introductions such as 'cuz', 'bro' and 'sweet', while other, older slang – such as 'drongo', 'skite' and 'rook' – gradually disappears.

Unsurprisingly, when it comes to language, New Zealanders have a special relationship with the letter Z. This predisposition was explored by Debra Daley in her 1996 novel *The Strange Letter Z*. In describing her own response to living away from New Zealand she explained that, 'Although I never felt overtly homesick for New Zealand, whenever my eye chanced upon a "Z" in any block of text, the "Z" leapt at me and interfered with my progress through the sentences. I suppose I was drawn to that letter in the peculiar expectation that the "Z" was signalling a mention of my country of origin … I began to collect, although only in the display cabinet of my mind, the letter zed. I liked the mark of Zorro, Roland Barthes' story "S/Z", cartoons whose balloons filled with "zzzz" indicating sleep, and languages, such as Japanese and Czech, crowded with zeds, where it was not a lonely letter at the terminus of the alphabet.'

GOOD HEALTH AND LONG LIFE

Hale and hearty at 73 years of age, Mr. J. K. Storrie of Oban Road, Brown's Bay, Auckland, drinks and enjoys three bottles of "Waitemata" every day. "I have done so for the past ten years," he says, "and feel a hundred per cent fit and well. I haven't had a day's illness in ten years, and expect to live to be a hundred."

Waitemata contributes to this happy state of living. Indeed it is a symbol of better and fuller living. Waitemata offers you pleasant companionship when you are alone: congenial fellowship when among friends, and a flourish to the hospitality that graces your home . . . Insist on Waitemata.

CS49

DOMINION BITTER
A WAITEMATA PRODUCT

Rugby, racing and beer (Desert Gold was one of the greatest racehorses to have run in New Zealand).

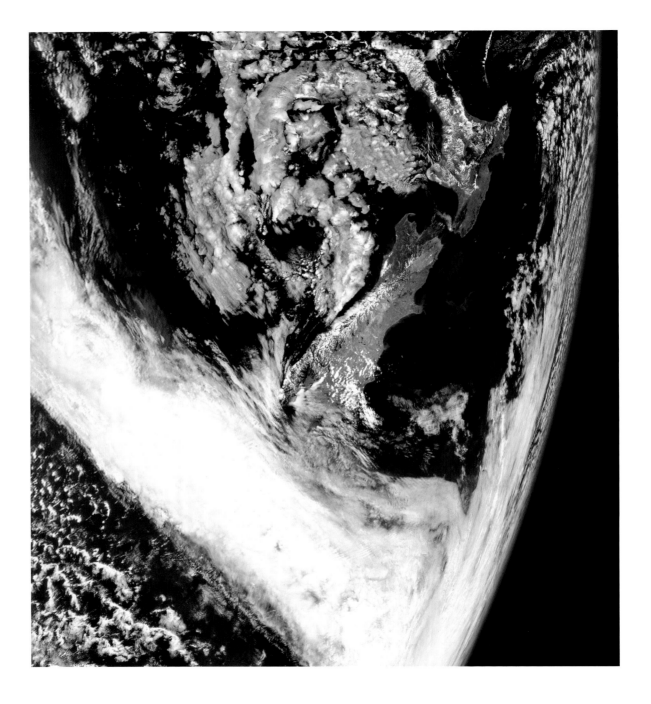

Land & Identity

New Zealand is similar in size to Japan, the British Isles, and the US state of Colorado. It consists of two main landmasses, which since the early nineteenth century have been known, rather unimaginatively, as North Island and South Island. The early Māori knew the North Island as Te Ika a Māui (the Fish of Māui), a reference to the legend of demigod Māui and his brothers fishing the land up from the sea. An alternative Māori name for the North Island, later applied to the whole country, was Aotearoa, usually translated as 'land of the long white cloud'. Aotearoa enjoyed further popularity in the late nineteenth century, appealing to the European appetite for ancient myths and legends, and today is a widely accepted alternative name for New Zealand.

The Māori knew the South Island as Te Wāi Pounamu (the Waters of Greenstone), a reference to the source of the distinctive stone, nephrite or jade, worked by Māori artists. In 2013 formal approval was given for Te Ika a Maui and Te Wāi Pounamu to be used as alternative names for the North and South islands.

The first European known to visit New Zealand was Dutchman Abel Tasman, who charted its west coast in 1642 believing it to be part of a great southern continent. His discovery appeared in later Dutch maps as Nieuw Zeeland, in honour of the Dutch province of Zeeland, which later became anglicised.

Europe gained a more accurate understanding of New Zealand thanks to Captain James Cook. In 1770, during the first of his three Pacific voyages, he circumnavigated this country in the *Endeavour*, sailing some 3800 kilometres and compiling the first complete chart of coastline. Although his chart had a few excusable errors - Banks Peninsula was believed to be an island and Stewart Island (which he named Cape South) was tentatively attached to the mainland - it was remarkably accurate and formed the basis of charts later produced by the British Admiralty.

Cook gave names to prominent features that were variously descriptive, reflected experiences of his crew or honoured influential individuals. Thus, Poverty Bay was so named because it offered Cook little of interest, and an inlet he sailed past in Northland became Doubtless Bay because it was

ABOVE *Aoraki/Mt Cook.*
RIGHT *During the early years of European settlement, the country was given a number of common names, among them 'Fernland'. At the same time the form of the silver fern or ponga was increasingly used in commerce and to represent New Zealand.*

'doubtless a bay'. On the west coast of the North Island Cook named a large mountain Egmont, after a First Lord of the Admiralty, rather overlooking the fact that it had long been known to Māori as Taranaki. Cook himself was also honoured, when in later years his name was given to Cook Strait, between the two main islands. In 1851 the country's highest peak, known to the Maori as Aoraki, was named Mt Cook. The mountain was officially renamed Aoraki/Mt Cook in 1998.

Cook had claimed New Zealand for Britain, and the publication of his voyages drew Europe's attention to the natural resources of the wider Pacific region. The informal European settlement of New Zealand began in the late 1700s, and on 6 February 1840 *Te Tiriti o Waitangi* (the Treaty of Waitangi) was signed between Māori and the Crown. This treaty, regarded as New Zealand's founding document, guaranteed Māori full possession of their land in exchange for their recognition of British sovereignty. New Zealand was a colony of Britain for the next 67 years, until 1907 when it became a dominion of the British Empire, alongside Australia, Canada and South Africa. This apparent elevation of status had little practical effect, but it did suggest an emerging sense of independent national identity.

New Zealand's loyalty to the Empire was demonstrated by its willingness to fight alongside Britain in the Anglo-Boer (or South African) War, of 1899-1902, and in the subsequent First and Second World Wars. New Zealand continued to be closely tied to Britain, and its economy remained largely dependent on a farming industry dominated by sheep. But by the 1960s things were beginning to change, especially following Britain's admission to the European Common Market (now the European Union)

in 1973. In addition to finding new markets for its produce, New Zealand's population was now becoming more ethnically diverse, with an increasing number of arrivals from the Pacific and, more recently, Asia.

New Zealand was the last habitable landmass on earth to be settled by humans. The first people to arrive here, some 700 years ago, found a land largely covered with dense forest. Those early Polynesian settlers, ancestors of the Māori, began the process of adjusting to and exploiting the new flora and fauna. Birds featured prominently in Māori myth and legend, and acted as messengers to the gods. They were also a source of food, in particular the large flightless moa which was hunted to extinction, probably by the eighteenth century.

New Zealand's rich birdlife was apparent to early European visitors. When Captain Cook's *Endeavour* was in Queen Charlotte Sound, at the north of the South Island, in January 1770, botanist Joseph Banks was woken by the dawn chorus of birds singing from shore, some 400 metres distant. As he described it in his journal: 'their voices were certainly the most melodious wild musick I have ever heard, almost imitating small bells but with the most tuneable silver sound imaginable …'

NEW ZEALAND is a Must!

THE WONDERLAND OF THE South Pacific

Sadly, such concerts of massed bird-song were soon under threat. From the mid-1800s, as the result of increasing immigration from Europe, much of the original forest of New Zealand was destroyed by fire and axe, and converted into farmland, while trees provided the timber to build houses for the new settlers. Prior to human settlement, the birds of New Zealand had evolved in isolation and without fear of mammalian predators, and the larger ground-dwelling species had become flightless. But since the arrival of humans, some 57 species of birds – about 40 per cent of the country's terrestrial stock – have become extinct, the result of their being hunted for food, forest clearance and the result of the introduction of such animals as rats, dogs and stoats.

To attract settlers to New Zealand, early eighteenth-century publicity pointed out the benefits of its soil and congenial climate, and the quality of its rivers and harbours. Later came recognition of the young colony's tourism potential, a main attraction being the geysers and bubbling mud pools of the thermal region in the central North Island. There followed in 1901 the establishment of a Tourist and Health Resorts Department, the first dedicated tourist department in the world. Early promotions focused on Māori life and culture, as could be seen in Rotorua, and the country's geographic attractions – its mountains, lakes and rivers which were favourably compared to those of Europe. For those who fancied the great outdoors, this was a 'sportsman's paradise', offering tramping and mountain-climbing, along with hunting and fishing, the latter activities

When writer Rudyard Kipling visited here in the 1890s, he was struck by the country's beauty. Milford Sound he thought the eighth wonder of the world; Auckland as famously, 'Last, loneliest, loveliest, exquisite, apart'.

enhanced by the introduction of various exotic game birds, animals and fish.

But as New Zealand was being converted into a farm, primarily to produce meat, wool and dairy products for Britain, little thought was given to the impact of the disappearance of its once extensive bush cover. Native forests had once protected the soil, and tree roots provided stability to hillsides. With their removal, however, rain was now able to begin the process of erosion, resulting in ugly slips scarring the landscape. In addition, introduced animals such as deer and possums trampled on and ate the plants and trees. The current population of some 30 million possums chomps its way through vast quantities of leaf buds, flowers and fruit in our native forests, and is also partial to birds' eggs, insects and snails.

By the 1960s there was growing awareness of the need for measures to protect New Zealand's natural environment. There were challenges to government policies, and controversies over such issues as forest clearance and the modification of lakes and rivers for the generation of electricity. In 1987 the need for the sustainable management of natural resources led to the formation of the Department of Conservation, which became responsible for the care and protection of all Crown land. This covers some 8 million hectares (about 30 per cent of the land area of New Zealand) and its domain includes native forests, tussocklands, alpine areas, lakes, maritime parks and reserves.

The most frequently debated symbol of New Zealand is its national flag, with its references to our early links with Britain. Known as the Blue Ensign it was officially adopted in 1902, but it was not this country's first flag.

In the 1830s New Zealand ships carrying goods to markets in Australia were required by British navigation law to fly a flag indicating their country

The flag of the United Tribes, adopted as the country's national flag, was superseded by the Union Jack following the signing of the Treaty of Waitangi in 1840. The particular flag of the United Tribes seen here was made on board the New Zealand Company ship the Tory *during its voyage to New Zealand.*

of origin. As a result, Australian authorities and a New Zealand-based missionary drew up three designs for such a flag, and these were presented to leading Māori representatives at Waitangi, in the Bay of Islands. They chose what became known as the Flag of the United Tribes, and from 1834 to 1840, when it was replaced by the Union Jack, it was recognised as New Zealand's first 'national flag', flown around the Bay of Islands and on ships trading around New Zealand and across the Tasman. The flag consisted of a red cross on a white background, with four stars of the Southern Cross – the prominent constellation visible in the Southern Hemisphere – set in the top left corner (known as the canton). Although it was later superseded, this flag remains important to the Māori of northern New Zealand.

By 1865 New Zealand was a colony of Britain

The Blue Ensign was first flown by colonial ships in the 1860s.

and new regulations required colonial ships to fly the British Blue Ensign with the Union Jack in the upper left corner as their maritime flag. New Zealand needed its own emblem to incorporate into this design, and again adopted the four stars of the Southern Cross. Towards the end of the century, an increasing awareness of national identity coupled with a surge of patriotism occasioned by New Zealand's support for Britain in the war in South Africa saw calls to make the Blue Ensign the flag the country flew on land as well. This was officially approved in March 1902.

The new flag went on to serve New Zealand well, but by the late twentieth century there were suggestions that the country might consider something more relevant and distinctive. Among the arguments for change was that there had long been confusion with Australia's flag, which also consists of the Union Jack and the Southern Cross against a blue ground. The only difference between the two national flags is the Australian representation of the constellation with five stars, while an additional large star symbolises the federation of the colonies of Australia.

In 1983 Austrian-born artist Friedensreich Hundertwasser, who lived in Northland, proposed a flag of his own design that depicted an unfurling koru, in the characteristic green of the New Zealand bush. A few years later, the approach of New Zealand's sesquicentennial in 1990 – marking the 150th anniversary of the signing of the Treaty of Waitangi and colonisation by Britain – triggered a new resurgence of discussion on national identity and the matter of the country's flag.

Most recently, over 2015 and 2016, New Zealanders were given the chance to vote on a new flag in a two-part referendum. In the first stage they were offered five alternatives for a new flag, and opted for a design with the silver fern and Southern Cross against a black and white background. When asked to choose between this design and the current national flag, the majority of voters decided to stick with the status quo. It seems inevitable that at some later date there will be a greater appetite for change but for now the old Blue Ensign continues to fly overhead.

In 1642 when Abel Tasman approached the South Island from the west, he recorded sighting 'a large land, uplifted high'. This land 'uplifted high' was the northern part of the Southern Alps, a creation, like so much of New Zealand's geology, of the country's constant seismic activity.

Earthquakes are a daily event in New Zealand; every year the country experiences over 14,000 such shakes, most of which are fortunately extremely minor. The reason for such a high number is all to do with the country's location. It lies within a geographical area known as the Ring of Fire, a belt of volcanoes and tectonic plate boundaries that line the Pacific Ocean and connect this country, Japan and the west coast of the Americas. New Zealand straddles two

tectonic plates – the Pacific and the Australian Plates – and where they meet, the top layer, or crust, can be put under immense pressure and rupture, causing a sudden release of energy. Depending on the amount of land displaced, this produces waves that spread outwards and are felt as earthquakes.

For this country's first inhabitants, the Māori, such movements of the land were caused by the travels of Rūaumoko, the god of earthquakes and volcanoes. For early European settlers, earthquakes were a continuing reminder of the shaky nature of these isles. In May 1840 there was a series of shocks centred on Port Nicholson, Wellington, and local residents experienced what a local newspaper described rather poetically as 'an undulatory motion of the earth'. Later that year the effect of another quake was likened to 'a heavily laden wagon passing upon a pavement'. These unsettling experiences continued, and in 1842 another earthquake, which lasted for about four seconds, was described as 'an upheaving of the earth'.

The early buildings erected here by European settlers were mostly made of wood. These had a natural flexibility, and an ability to withstand earthquakes. By comparison, during an earthquake in Wellington in 1848, buildings made of brick and masonry collapsed, and so their replacements were constructed in timber. As a result the town suffered less damage during the next major tremor, the Wairarapa earthquake of 1855, which was the most powerful ever recorded in New Zealand. Not so lucky were Napier and Hastings, which in 1931 were devastated by this country's worst ever natural disaster, the Hawke's Bay Earthquake (also known as the Napier Earthquake). It resulted in 258 deaths, caused by collapsing buildings and fires which spread rapidly when water supplies were cut and the main streets were filled with rubble, obstructing efforts of the fire brigades. The earthquake dramatically altered the local geography, lifting and causing the draining of low-lying land that later became the Hawke's Bay Airport. After the earthquake Napier was rebuilt, and

Christchurch Normal School, destroyed in the earthquake of 2011.

a large number of new buildings were designed in the then fashionable Art Deco style.

More recently, Christchurch in the South Island has experienced two major earthquakes, in 2010 and 2011. Although the second earthquake was not as powerful as its predecessor, it occurred on a shallow fault line closer to the city and its effect was more destructive. Many buildings already damaged in the earlier shake were brought down, and 185 people lost their lives.

The country's propensity for earthquakes was the motivation for the lead rubber bearing (LRB) seismic isolation device invented by Auckland-born Bill Robinson. Incorporated into the foundations of buildings, these ingenious devices are designed to reduce their motion by absorbing the kinetic

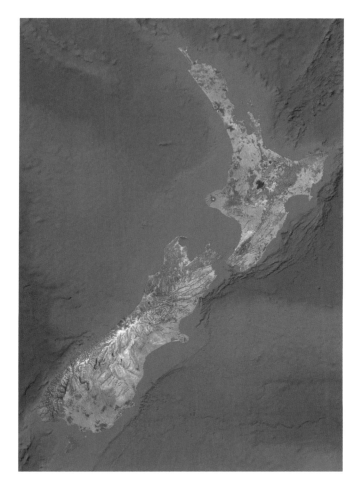

Mind the gap – a land riven by active faults.

energy of an earthquake when it strikes. They are now installed in Parliament Buildings in Wellington as well as in buildings and bridges around the world.

The national identity of New Zealand has also been colourfully expressed by its home-grown musicians.

The sounds of the natural world were an inspiration for early Māori music, produced with trumpets of conch shells and a range of flutes which included the kōauau, the nguru (which could be played with the mouth or nose) and the torpedo-shaped pūtōrino. Another distinctive feature of traditional Māori music was the unaccompanied voice, as in the waiata, a song of love or lament.

Early European settlers to New Zealand brought pianos and other instruments, and the country was soon introduced to military, brass and Scottish pipe band music. From the early 1900s the country also received regular visits by overseas performers, from Dame Nellie Melba in 1903 to Yehudi Menuhin in 1935. This period saw the growth of musical compositions with a distinctly local flavour, their titles ranging from 'I've Lost My Heart in Maoriland' and 'Beneath the Maori Moon' to 'Waitemata Waltz' and 'Goodbye Taranaki'.

Around 1915 Māori words were added to a tune that appears to have been composed in Australia, and after further modifications the song became the 'Haere Rā Waltz Song'. English singer Gracie Fields learnt it during her 1945 visit to New Zealand, recording it as 'Now is the Hour' (her manager is credited with changing the first line, which gave the new title) and it achieved worldwide popularity in 1948.

The following year, 1949, a 78 rpm disc featuring the song 'Blue Smoke', written by Ruru Karaitiana and sung by Pixie Williams, became the first record to be wholly produced in New Zealand from composition to pressing. Karaitiana wrote the song in 1940 while on a troopship off the coast of Africa, inspired by the sight of some passing smoke. Back in New Zealand his recording of the song topped the nation's radio hit parades for six weeks, while it was also covered by overseas artists including Dean Martin.

In the mid-1950s New Zealand succumbed to a new musical revolution, rock 'n' roll, which initially arrived from America. But this country had its own exponents in the form of Country and Western singer Johnny Cooper – known as the 'Maori Cowboy' – and the more commercially successful Raetihi-born Johnny Devlin, backed by The Devils.

New Zealand's most successful home-grown pop/rock band was Split Enz, formed in Auckland in 1972. Ahead of the times with their zany costumes and performances, they also included local references in their songs. 'Six Months in a Leaky Boat' (1982) alluded to the time it took early settlers to sail from Europe to the Antipodes and included the patriotic line 'Ao-tea-roa, rugged individual', while the autobiographical 'Haul Away' (1982) acknowledged Tim Finn's home town of Te Awamutu. In 1985, following the break-up of Split Enz, Tim's younger brother Neil formed Crowded House in Melbourne. The band achieved international success with 'Don't Dream It's Over' and 'Something So Strong' (both 1987) and, along with Split Enz, is now claimed by both New Zealand and Australia.

From the late 1950s a spate of songs examined aspects of the Kiwi way of life, among them Peter Cape's 'Taumaranui on the Main Trunk Line' (1957) and 'Down the Hall on a Saturday Night' (1958), and Rod Derrett's 'Rugby, Racing and Beer' (c.1965). The Howard Morrison Quartet added to this genre with their home-made parodies of other peoples' songs, most notably 1960s 'My Old Man's an All Black', based on Lonnie Donegan's 'My Old Man's a Dustman'. Significantly, the Quartet's version included a reference to the controversial decision not to include Māori in the national rugby team selected to play in South Africa in 1959. The light-hearted perspective on national idiosyncrasies was maintained in the 1970s by John Clarke, otherwise known as Fred Dagg, with his 'We Don't Know How

Lucky We Are' and his 'Gumboot Song', the latter a reworking of Billy Connolly's 'Welly Boot Song', which itself was a modification of a traditional song, 'The Work of the Weavers'.

In 1982 a growing anti-nuclear campaign in New Zealand was reflected in 'French Letter' by the Auckland-based multicultural reggae group The Herbs. Their protest at French testing in the South Pacific spent 11 weeks on the New Zealand charts. Two years later, 'Poi E', sung entirely in Māori by the Patea Maori Club, topped the national charts. It was written by Māori linguist and composer Ngoi Pēwhairangi, with music scored by Dalvanius Prime.

The official song of national pride is 'God Defend New Zealand', based on a poem written by Thomas Bracken. Set to music by John Joseph Woods, 'God Defend New Zealand' became our national hymn in 1940 and then in 1977 was raised in rank to second national anthem, alongside 'God Save the Queen'. Bracken was also responsible for applying the label 'God's Own Country' (often shortened to Godzone) to New Zealand, which he used in the title of a poem about the country, and the phrase became popularised by New Zealand's Prime Minister Richard Seddon (1845-1906). According to one source, 'God's Own Country' was first used in Britain 'to describe Yorkshire and subsequently has been associated with lesser territories …'

Fred Dagg – 'We don't know how lucky we are.'

The Kiwi

With only a small population compared to other countries, New Zealanders are something of a rarity, like the bird we take our nickname from. Not only a rarity, the kiwi is quite unlike any other bird. To describe it as an ornithological oddity would be an understatement. In addition to being flightless and nocturnal, the kiwi's list of unusual features include nostrils at the tip of its long beak, feathers that are more like hair than feathers, and eggs that are unusually large in relation to body size. Prior to human settlement this country had no land mammals except for bats, and so the kiwi occupied the ecological niche that elsewhere is filled by such animals as hedgehogs and badgers.

The kiwi is a member of the ratite group of birds, which includes the emu, ostrich and New Zealand's own extinct moa. It is now believed that the kiwi evolved from a small bird that flew to New Zealand some tens of millions of years ago. The kiwi held a special place in Māori culture, and its feathers were used for cloaks, kahu kiwi, which were usually

OPPOSITE *The legs say it all.*

reserved for chiefs. It was also eaten at times by Māori. One of the few Europeans thought to have eaten kiwi was author Rudyard Kipling, although it is considered that the bird he ate was more likely to have been a weka. While touring the country in 1891 he recorded that, 'I was given for dinner a roast bird with a skin like pork crackling, but it had no wings nor any trace of any. It was a kiwi - an apteryx. I ought to have saved its skeleton, for few men have eaten apteryx.'

With the arrival of European settlers and the conversion of the bush country into farmland, the kiwi came under threat from loss of habitat and from introduced predators. At the same time, from the middle of nineteenth century, it also began its lengthy career as a national symbol.

Up until the early 1900s cartoonists had used various symbols to represent New Zealand, among them representations of the fern and the moa, while at the same time the silver fern was gaining

popularity to identify its citizens, and especially its sporting representatives. It was during the First World War that New Zealand soldiers overseas began to be referred to as Kiwis. The bird had already appeared on military badges, but the connection between kiwi and New Zealanders was to be strengthened by the kiwi's appearance on small round tins of boot polish much in demand by the military. Ironically, Kiwi boot polish originated in Australia (in 1906), but was named for the inventor's wife's homeland.

In the years following the First World War the kiwi consolidated its position and became unchallenged as unofficial national symbol. While it has graced the nation's banknotes, coins and postage stamps, unlike the silver fern and Southern Cross (which appear on the nation's coat of arms) the kiwi has not had the same level of governmental profile. However it has been used – in name and depiction – with innumerable commercial enterprises including a bacon company, a national lottery, the horse that won the Melbourne Cup in 1983, and a small brown and hairy fruit previously known in this country as the Chinese gooseberry.

The kiwi has proved a remarkably successful symbol, but the future of the bird is uncertain. Human settlement of New Zealand brought about the destruction of its natural habitat, while the introduction of predators such as cats, dogs, possums and stoats threatened both the bird and its eggs. The declining kiwi population was apparent by 1929 when an Auckland newspaper reported that an effort was being made to raise its profile by exhibiting a live specimen at a forthcoming poultry show.

There are considered to be five species of kiwi, including the North Island brown, the great spotted and the little spotted. Kiwi had received official protection in 1896, but realisation that it might be following the moa down the road to extinction led to the establishment of a national recovery plan in 1991. Initiatives have involved the artificial incubation of eggs, and the release of chicks on predator-free offshore islands. A further government-funded rescue plan was announced in early 2016, when the national kiwi population was then estimated at 68,000 and declining at the rate of 2 per cent per year. New Zealanders have a responsibility to ensure the livelihood of their kiwi, the most original of birds, and one which has contributed so much to their own sense of identity.

ABOVE *A bird quite unlike any other.*
OPPOSITE *The Kiwi Milk Bar, Wellington, late 1950s.*

ABOVE *Kiwi boot polish originated in Australia (in 1906).*
LEFT *The biggest commercial representations of kiwis were those used to advertise Hutton's Kiwi Bacon. These steel and fibreglass models were installed during the 1960s on top of the company's buildings in the main centres and over the years became much-loved landmarks of those cities' skylines. 'So long a part of their local environment,' as photographer Geoffrey Short has remarked, 'that only strangers would think it odd that somehow kiwis might be a source of bacon'.*

Bred in the Bone

For nearly as long as this country has been 'Godzone', it has also been hailed as a good place to bring up children. This was certainly the case from the middle of last century onwards, and children here are fortunate indeed to live in a land that enjoys an abundance of fresh air, sunlight and space, and with the wilderness of hills and coast never far away.

By the early 1940s, New Zealand was at the forefront in the world when it came to care for infants and children: free dental and medical care, and free milk in schools were just some of the benefits of their early years, beginning in the safe hands of Plunket soon after birth.

The Plunket Society was founded in 1907 and named for Lady Plunket, whose support for the organisation ensured it a high profile. At the time

Lady Victoria Alexandrina Plunket, wife of the Governor of New Zealand Lord Plunket, and a passionate advocate of the organisation that had been formed by Dunedin doctor Frederic Truby King and his wife Isabella with the aim of helping mothers and saving babies and to which the Plunket name was lent.

the country's record on infant care was abysmal, and before long Plunket had become an integral part of the country's health system. The nationwide organisation offering preventative care has succeeded in large measure due to a unique support network of volunteers.

Led by Sir Truby King, the organisation's philosophy for infant and child care stressed the importance of fresh air, sunshine, diet and exercise. Plunket held that when the child went to school, the time spent within halls of learning should be also be physically beneficial. Early twentieth-century primary schools provided large areas of playing fields while classrooms were airy and filled with light. The buildings often featured verandahs, with large, glazed, folding doors that spanned one wall to let in a maximum amount of sunlight and fresh air.

As well as learning their three Rs, generations of young Kiwis grew up learning the ABCs of their country's natural world. The covers of their school exercise books and writing pads displayed images of our native birds as painted by Johannes Keulemans, which had originally appeared in Walter Buller's

NORTH ISLAND KIWI
Apteryx mantelli

Birds of New Zealand
AN OLYMPIC PRODUCTION

Manufactured by
OLYMPIC STATIONERY LTD.
Series No. 6   Subject No. 46

SCHOOL WRITING PAD
36 leaves 10 x 8 **9G** ruled 2 spaces to inch

Reproduced by courtesy of THE DOM INION MUSEUM, from the 'BIRDS OF NEW ZEALAND' by Sir Walter Buller.

ABOVE *A school writing pad of the 1960s featuring New Zealand's unique natural history.*
RIGHT *This won't hurt . . .*

books in the nineteenth century, and familiarised children with New Zealand's unique birdlife. Similar osmotic absorption took place with regard to our native trees, this time by way of wooden pencil cases and rulers inlaid with slivers of wood from mataī, rimu, tawa, beech, kauri, pūriri and others, an innovation of Sovereign Woodworkers in Wanganui.

Further positive reinforcement was to be had in school mottos (although these were often somewhat obscure for young brains, such as 'Sacrifice Before Self') borne on boards high up on the school buildings and whose influence it was hoped would adhere whenever pupils raised their eyes. The frequent presence of straw, string and feathers poking out from behind the board, where sparrows nested warm and dry, may have distracted from the effect, but then it provided a little nature study as well.

Less uplifting was the school dental clinic, better known as the Murder House. Often sited at the end

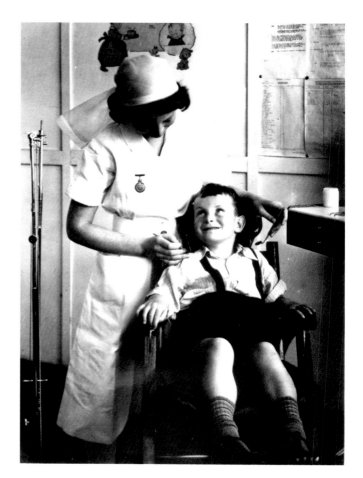

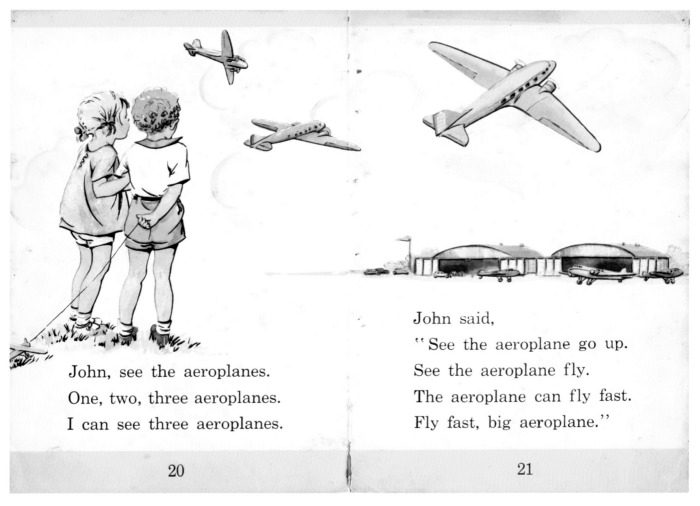

John, see the aeroplanes.
One, two, three aeroplanes.
I can see three aeroplanes.

20

John said,
"See the aeroplane go up.
See the aeroplane fly.
The aeroplane can fly fast.
Fly fast, big aeroplane."

21

The Janet and John *series of readers ('Look, John, look!'), together with the Department of Educations' School Journal and A.W.B. Powell's* Native Animals of New Zealand, *were the most memorable of the publications put in front of growing Kiwis.*

of a lonely pathway some distance from the main cluster of buildings - in order, one imagined, that the screams of the victims would not carry to the classrooms - pupils were called there twice yearly. Messengers bearing the fateful summons would enter a classroom to speak the awful words to the teacher, and if you were really unlucky the electric drill would be out of commission and the dental nurse would

be using one of the old-style treadle-powered drills whose much slower speed served to drag out the torture.

For anyone at primary school in New Zealand from the late 1930s until the late 1960s, an enduring memory is that of school milk. All across the country at 10 o'clock the rattling of half-pint bottles in wire crates signalled morning playtime. School milk had its origins in the Depression. The widespread poverty of the period had led to undernourishment among thousands of children while at the same time there was a large surplus of milk available as the result of reduced economic activity. Among the voices raised in favour of a free milk scheme to address this situation was that of British playwright and critic George Bernard Shaw. Like many other international commentators of the time, Shaw saw New Zealand as a kind of social laboratory in which the absence of class, an even spread of wealth, a gentle climate and ready access to open spaces were producing a fair and just society of fit and healthy individuals. While on a visit here in 1934 he argued that 'a little loss on milk does not matter. It is of enormous importance that all your children should have plenty of milk and that the next generation should be a generation reared from first-class children.'

Shaw was lauded during his month-long visit to New Zealand with crowds at his meetings hanging on his opinions and criticisms of everything from school milk to tourism; when in Rotorua he visited

OPPOSITE *The 10 o'clock swill. Schoolchildren down their half-pint daily ration of milk.*
RIGHT *Health camps (for which money was raised each year through the sale of health stamps) were another initiative that put the country at the forefront when it came to care for the child.*

one of the local thermal areas and was so impressed with its fire and brimstone he likened it to 'Hell's Gate' – by which name it continues to be known today. The free school milk scheme eventually began in 1937, introduced by the Labour Government, and lasted until 1967 when it was dropped for reasons of cost, and also because there were now questions about the health benefits of milk.

While children of the times diligently drank their milk each morning (hoping it hadn't become sickly warm during the hours it had remained outside in the milk stands, which often did not provide adequate shade from the sun), there was also the

attraction of other dietary supplements along the lines of penny-sweets – such as milk bottles, wine gums, jelly airplanes and pineapple chunks, as well as Buzz Bars and chocolate slabs. The latter had evolved from the hand-moulded slabs of chocolate made in the days before machines, the slabs having indented divisions so they could be broken off into smaller pieces by the shopkeeper and then weighed for sale. The advent of moulding machines saw the slab size standardised.

More chocolate was to be found in the shape of Jaffas. They were not only good to eat but also useful in a number of ways when it came to the Saturday afternoon movies. For rolling down the inclined wooden floors in the old cinemas for example; or for letting loose when the film whipped up overwhelming excitement or, conversely, was dead boring – a barrage of Jaffas directed at the screen often helped. While there isn't a lot of that behaviour these days, Jaffas still feature; an annual competition in Dunedin sees them in their thousands rolled down the steepest street in the world.

Children's play at that time was generally more boisterous, given the absence of the frequent present-day obsession with overly bureaucratic health and safety regulations. You climbed trees, went to school barefoot (stubbing toes and becoming familiar with mercurochrome), played bullrush and other potentially injurious games, and learnt to handle risk and make judgements. You grew up.

LEFT . . . *the attraction of other dietary supplements.*
OPPOSITE *Jaffas . . . not just for the eating. A scene from the annual Cadbury Jaffa Race in Dunedin.*

The Quarter-Acre Paradise

If an Englishman's house is his castle, then for the New Zealander it was his paradise, as famously described in 1972 in *The Half-Gallon Quarter-Acre Pavlova Paradise* by Austin Mitchell who, before he became a British Labour Party politician, had lectured in history and sociology in New Zealand. His book likened New Zealand to a vision of heaven on earth.

Housing's traditional quarter-acre plot (1000 square metres for the metrically minded) has been hugely formative in the lives of Kiwis, providing ample space in which to do things, for a shed or a chook-house, and corners in which to store a boat and an old car, in addition to more prosaic areas for the clothesline and gardens. Australian writer Robin Ingram has written of our backyards: 'Dads had a few rows of spuds and spinach and Mums a corner [for] flowers. And when domestic strife broke out over such complex issues as the way the hose was coiled, Dads would withdraw to musty back sheds containing tricycles and badminton sets from Christmases past. The back shed was the refugee camp for the Dad in strife … a refuge from which to ponder life as a bastard until tea was ready.'

As a child there was space to explore, to stretch out, to make things and absorb basic yardcraft. There was ample room for rampant do-it-yourself activities, especially on the weekends when the nation's backyards resounded with the whirr of mowers, the whine of power tools, the repetition of hammer blows and the engine noise from a procession of trailers going to and from the tip and builders' supply depots. Concrete paths, new fences, decks, painting, renovations and the ubiquitous lawnmowing are all grist to the mill of weekend industry. A lot of that activity has to do with the country's main domestic building construction that uses wood and corrugated iron. Older houses in particular threaten a return to the soil if it were not for suburban men and women working to slow entropy and restore order.

Lawns. There's always the lawns to do. New Zealand, with its moist temperate climate, grows grass well. To the degree that the country's main earnings are derived from the very highly efficient business of converting grass into dairy products, wool and meat. In suburbia meanwhile, with no beasts to keep the grass down, the lawn becomes something of a

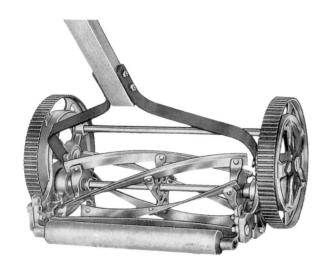

When we weren't mowing, we were planting things, and for many years Yates has been a name synonymous with New Zealand gardening. Arthur Yates arrived here in 1879 from Manchester. His family in England were seed merchants and it was while working on farms during his first few years in this country that Yates saw the opportunities that existed in supplying seeds locally. In 1883 he founded Arthur Yates and Company. Like another great Kiwi success story – Edmonds baking powder – the Yates business gave rise to a book, the *Yates' Garden Guide* that has been the bible for New Zealand's home gardeners. Now in its 79th edition, the *Garden Guide* has sold over one million copies since first published in 1895.

preoccupation for many householders.

Our most famous lawnmower had its origins in 1910 when two young New Zealand engineers, Reuben Porter and Harold Mason, went into business together in Auckland to manufacture pumps and engines. But it was to be in the manufacture of lawnmowers (push ones at first, and later two-stroke) that 'Masport' became a household name. The face of Antipodean lawnmowing was radically and rotarily altered one afternoon in 1952 in Concord, New South Wales when Mervyn Victor Richardson decided to connect a small petrol motor to a rotary blade. Conventional cylindrical mowers are mostly defeated by the kind of coarse lawn grasses that dominate in Australia and New Zealand and the greater cutting power of the rotary blade proved an immediate hit. Richardson opened a factory in the following year to manufacture his 'Victa' mower. New Zealand-made versions soon followed.

OPPOSITE *The lawn becomes something of a preoccupation.*

Seeing is Believing

Preserve Summer
Sweets for Winter
Needs

Use Only
"AGEE" JARS
For Best Results

Obtainable at all leading stores
throughout New Zealand

Manufactured by
Australian Glass
Manufacturers Co. Ltd.
PENROSE, AUCKLAND

ABOVE *Putting up bottled fruits and vegetables was once part of the seasonal round. Nearly everybody preserved something.* RIGHT *If at first you don't succeed, call it something else.*

Characteristic of the New Zealand home garden in warmer districts are crops such as kiwifruit, tamarillo (once known as tree tomato, though that name has gone the way of Chinese gooseberry), feijoa, passionfruit and kūmara. The kūmara was among a number of food crops, including yam, taro and the gourd, brought to New Zealand by the first Polynesian settlers. Kūmara was the most successful of them, and indeed became the most important cultivated crop for Māori. It was grown throughout the North Island and in the South Island as far south as Banks Peninsula. Further south the climate is too cold.

The Chinese gooseberry was introduced to home gardeners in the 1920s. Half a century later New Zealand commercial growers were exporting them to the world, renamed as kiwifruit. Both the name change and the drive to export were the work of wholesale fruit and vegetable company Turners and Growers. They had identified kiwifruit, with its ability to keep well in cold storage - allowing crops to be sent overseas by seafreight - as one that could be successfully exported.

At a company meeting in 1959, the name 'kiwifruit' was coined by Turners and Growers to replace 'Chinese gooseberry'; a change made in response to problems the company was having in trying to launch the fruit on the huge and potentially profitable American market. US import regulations placed a higher tariff on 'gooseberries' than other fruits not specifically provided for, and kiwifruit wasn't a gooseberry. It's also been suggested that American importers may have been wary of anything bearing the name 'Chinese', as this was still close to the time of the 'red scare' in the USA.

Any story about the New Zealand garden wouldn't be complete without mention of that other rotary device, the rotary clothesline. Early Kiwi clotheslines were linear affairs, the lines being cords or galvanised wire (the 1930s housewife was advised to check the wire line for rust) that were raised and lowered using a notched pole or paling. Salvation was once again at hand from Australia, this time in the form of the Hills Hoist, a revolving clothesline made by Lance Hill for his wife in the 1940s. Not only was the line now able to be rotated to catch the sun and breeze, but hanging out the washing could be done from one spot. New Zealand-made versions of the Hills Hoist design were soon sprouting in backyards across the country.

With all this activity going on in the backyard, a shed was needed in which to store items, or to escape to. Throwing up a shed in the backyard was straightforward as there always seemed to be a few old sheets of corrugated iron about the place. Along with 4×2 (now 100×50) framing and weatherboards, it is the great New Zealand building material: a simple and effective covering for roofs; perfect for forming chimneys, sheds and fences; useful in suppressing weeds; and of course essential for making water tanks if you live in smaller towns, out in the countryside or at the coast and nowhere near a mains supply.

    Imported at first, corrugated iron was soon being manufactured locally, galvanised for rust resistance. When used for roofing it was usually painted a red iron oxide, or a more fade-proof 'permanent' green.

We Are What We Eat

Popular culture is also shaped by what we eat, so it's little surprise then that, living in a country of milk and meat since the days of colonisation, our mealtime thoughts should start with meat pies, ice cream and cheese.

Chesdale cheese, smooth-textured processed cheese of smoky taste, dates back to the time when home refrigeration was non-existent and Chesdale had the virtue of surviving in the cupboard without the need to be kept cool. Ordinary cheese might sweat, become oily, dry out, crack, grow mould and start to smell once it had been cut, but not Chesdale. Originally produced as a block, its foil-wrapped triangles and individual slices were a staple of school lunches and picnics.

Promotion of Chesdale has for many years involved a couple of rural types, Ches and Dale, and also contributed a jingle that became part of the Kiwi repertoire, brought out when there'd been a few drinks and no one could remember the words to anything else:

OPPOSITE *Ches and Dale.*

We are the boys from down on the farm
We really know our cheese
There's much better value in Chesdale,
it never fails to please
Chesdale slices thinly, never crumbles, there's no waste
And boy it's got a mighty taste,
Chesdale cheese – it's finest cheddar, made better!

PARAPARAUMU BEACH   S.C.SMITH PHOTO   No 2

New Zealanders love their ice cream as well, and have established themselves at the top of the world rankings for ice cream eaters. The first such local confections were hand-churned and sold from handcarts. Later, when milk bars had come into being, ice cream was made and sold on the premises. If this ice cream had any kind of brand name at all, it tended to take the name of the milk bar in which it was made. Later, when ice cream became more of a manufacturing concern and was made in factories, many of those original names were carried over, among them Everest, Arctic, Egmont, Frosty Jack and Tip Top.

Tip Top, the local giant in ice cream, grew from such characteristic small beginnings. In the 1930s the then manager of the Royal ice cream company in Dunedin and one of his customers decided they would go into business for themselves. While searching for a name for their new enterprise the two partners, seated in a restaurant, overheard a fellow diner use a then common expression – 'tip-top' – in his praise of the restaurant's service. The two partners had their name and now, armed with their own recipe and premises in Wellington, they began offering the public something new in the form of an ice cream shop in Manners Street selling solely ice creams and milkshakes – New Zealand's very first milk bar. By the end of the 1930s Tip Top milk bars had spread from Wellington to the lower half of the North Island, and to Nelson and Blenheim.

A favourite ice cream flavour with Kiwis is hokey-pokey, a blend of vanilla base and pieces of toffee, which Tip Top added to its range in the 1950s. While the idea of adding toffee to ice cream wasn't new – in the USA for instance, so-called 'candy' flavours were common at this time, and to this day there are ice creams similar to our hokey-pokey such as 'butter brickle' – what was unique was the distinctive taste given by the recipe used here for the toffee. This involved caramelising sugar and adding baking soda, resulting in hokey-pokey's familiar honeycomb structure. A patent for the recipe had been filed in the late 1890s and hokey-pokey had become a popular sweet in New Zealand long before it was added to ice cream.

Initially, Tip Top made their hokey-pokey toffee in large sheets which were then broken up, using hammers, into small pieces suitable for the ice cream blend. These would occasionally jam up the machinery however, and eventually the hokey-pokey was made in the standardised nuggets seen today that suit modern high-volume production.

Ice cream improved the flavour of milkshakes as well, and these were a standard of dairies and takeaway places – many of them using the chrome and green milkshake machines made by US company Hamilton Beach. Today it's regrettably a case of the disappearing creaming soda and other flavoured milkshakes, as fewer businesses are prepared to give space to the cartons of bulk ice cream or to put time and effort into making up milkshakes when milk drinks can be stocked in chill cabinets.

'It must be Wattie's!' That line from the radio jingle, in the pre-television days when radio was king, helped Wattie's to become a household name, and the company, J. Wattie Canneries, grow into one of the country's largest commercial concerns. It was all down to James Wattie's vision of a New Zealand self-sufficient in canned fruit and vegetables, an ambition that had been spurred by seeing the fruit and vegetable bounty of his Hawke's Bay region literally rotting on the ground for want of a preserving facility.

Sir Edmund Hillary chooses WEET-BIX

Sir Edmund Hillary took Weet-Bix with him on his famous Himalayan expedition. For the same reason, too — because Weet-Bix is so delicious, so full of nourishing goodness, so quick and easy to serve it's with the New Zealand Antarctic expedition. Have your Weet-Bix with hot milk. It's the perfect winter breakfast.

And here's another Weet-Bix scoop —

the story of flight on 50 full-colour picture cards

Fifty free full-colour cards tell the exciting story of the "Evolution of Flight". There are two cards in every large 24-ounce packet of Weet-Bix; one in the 12-ounce size. Start collecting them today.

Not just a breakfast for mountaineers but also the name ('weetbix') some climbers use to refer to loose, shattered rock.

Founded in 1934, Wattie's cannery was a success from the outset, and in the following decades the Wattie's name became synonymous with canned peaches, tomato sauce, fruit salad, asparagus and peas, as well as baked beans and spaghetti. And innovation and lateral thinking was always at the fore, as when it came to producing free-flow frozen peas. Frozen peas were first sold in solid blocks and, keen to be the first company to sell the free-flow version – in time for the Christmas of 1958 – the company suddenly had to resort to a spot of needs-must when the newly commissioned equipment was delayed. Wattie's instead had the peas frozen in trays which were then tipped out onto a big stainless steel table where staff hit them with mallets to separate them and produce a manual version of free-flow peas.

The national impact of Wattie's and its products was recognised in the 1960s by the following ditty from a university revue, sung to the tune of 'Land of Hope and Glory': *Land of fern and paua / Nestled by the sea / Peaches, peas and baked beans / Canned by James Wattie!*

If it's breakfast-time then you're likely to be one of the millions who start the day with a bowl of Weet-Bix. Weet-Bix is consumed by the tonne every day, amounting to hundreds of millions of the biscuits each year.

This health-conscious breakfast goes back to the nineteenth century when the 'Sanitarium' name was adopted by a health food company in Michigan in the US, which extended its business to New Zealand in 1900. Some years later Sanitarium purchased a company here called Grain Products and thereby became the owner of a grain flake biscuit called Weet-Bix. They're not just popular but versatile as well – you can eat Weet-Bix hot or cold and some people simply spread them with jam or Marmite. As 'the perfect winter breakfast', Weet-Bix had the distinction of accompanying Sir Edmund Hillary on his Himalayan and Antarctic expeditions.

There is a rich Weet-Bix subculture that includes people trying to consume the greatest number at a single sitting (the record is around 38, with milk, inside 40 minutes), while eating the biscuits dry, without the assistance of milk or other liquid, is perhaps the toughest challenge there is. The cardboard of the carton has always contributed a

Hot meat pies even in the trenches: New Zealand soldiers of the 2nd Otago Battalion collect food rations from a makeshift kitchen in Selles, France, in 1917. Daily supplies of meat pies and sausage rolls were issued to the troops and it was recorded that in every action in which the Battalion took part, 'these dainties' were rushed to them even in the foremost trenches, 'often under severe shelling'.

variety of uses as well, from making up emergency gaskets for old motorcycles to lining the soles of shoes.

Later in the day you'll probably want to grab a meat pie, one of the 60 million or so we get through as a nation each year. If there was a prize for the

If there was a prize for the single most 'Kiwi' item of cuisine then it would probably have to go to the meat pie.

Ballerina Anna Pavlova performed in New Zealand in 1926 at the age of 45, arriving in Auckland in late May and then touring the country. In this photo she is seen posing with some of the locals.

most iconic 'Kiwi' contribution to popular cuisine in these islands then it would have to go to the meat pie. A lunchtime legend and a staple of dairies, home bakeries and school tuck shops, the pie is the original fast food. While today's range extends to the likes of venison and sundried tomatoes, feta and pork, and bacon and caraway seeds, still dominant are the basic steak and mince pies, not forgetting steak and pepper.

At the end of the culinary day you might decide on barbecue for dinner. While not a Kiwi invention itself, the pre-barbecue onion dip that goes with the salt and vinegar chips certainly is. It was the innovation of Rosemary Dempsey in the 1960s when she was employed in the test kitchen of Nestlé, makers of both the reduced cream and dried onion soup mix from which the dip is concocted. Prior to

the dip, neither product was a great seller on its own until Rosemary had the brainwave of combining them. This eureka moment resulted in an instant classic of addictive texture and consistency just right with chips.

By now your average Kiwi is ready for dessert, and if it's a special occasion this might involve pavlova. The origin of this particular meringue and cream concoction stems from the tour through Australasia in the 1920s by Russian ballerina Anna Pavlova. The subject of whether this dish originated in New Zealand or Australia has long been the subject of debate – though only by Australians. The truth is of course that pavlova is a New Zealand creation. It was first made by the chef of a Wellington hotel who, during the New Zealand leg of Pavlova's tour, came up with a cream and fruit-topped meringue in an attempt to recreate the look of the dancer's dress, which was a tutu draped in roses made from green silk. Thus the pavlova's meringue case was covered in whipped cream for the tutu and slices of Chinese gooseberry (as they were then, now kiwifruit) to echo those green silk roses. The dancer's biographer Keith Money described the original recipe – with the only permissible fruit flavours being passionfruit in the cream and kiwifruit slices on top (not peaches or

Today, L&P is produced using plain water with the addition of the mineral salts that gave the original its taste.

The hugely popular flat white coffee is the subject of further culinary rivalry between Kiwis and our trans-Tasman cousins, but in this case it is more likely to be an instance of great minds thinking alike. Developed in the 1990s, the flat white is now making its way into cafés internationally. It's the coffee everyone likes. Indeed it can also be argued that it has played not a little part in a civilising role in parts of New Zealand's hinterland. In places where once there was only a home cookery or public bar, the flat white-driven café has provided a real community meeting place.

Home baking was the mainstay for many years of the household provision of biscuits, scones and cakes, and not a lot of baking can be done without baking powder. While difficult to imagine today, there was great competition among manufacturers to supply a baking powder that was effective and reliable.

strawberries) – as 'a brilliant simulacrum of Pavlova's personality' and of her performing style 'which was invariably praised for its subtlety and strangeness'.

To wash this all down, choose from L&P, 'world famous in New Zealand', or, if you'd prefer, a flat white coffee.

L&P (shortened from the original 'Lemon & Paeroa') is a soft drink that originated with the natural mineral water of a spring in the township of Paeroa. Around the end of the nineteenth century, residents of the town found that the spring water provided a refreshing drink, especially with lemon added. Before long the Paeroa Natural Mineral Water Company had come into being. This business was later taken over by an aerated water-bottling company that began shipping wooden casks of the water to its Auckland factory, where it was flavoured and bottled.

The life-affirming rays of the morning sun was an ancient symbol, and popular with manufacturers in the nineteenth century. For Edmonds' customers the golden sunburst suggested reliability, while a display of successful baking on the label provided oven-tested evidence of the product's efficacy. In addition, a pennant on the label carried the bold claim: 'Public / Opinion / Once Used / Always / Used / Try It'.

Staff outside the TJ Edmonds Ltd Sure to Rise building in Christchurch. As business boomed, the company had outgrown its original premises and in 1922 moved into this new factory and offices on Christchurch's Ferry Road. The building was placed within one of the first factory gardens in New Zealand, allowing staff to enjoy beautiful surroundings. The new premises with its 'Sure to Rise' slogan over the façade and its award-winning gardens soon became a local landmark.

In the late 1870s Lyttelton grocer Thomas Edmonds decided to tackle the matter of reliability by selling a powder mixed to his own formula. When a doubting customer asked if it would work, Edmonds gave his guarantee that with his product her baking was 'sure to rise'. With that comment a successful commercial slogan was born, leading to the now famous Edmonds rising sun label. Nearly a century-and-a-half later that image qualifies as one of New Zealand's best-known and most durable commercial trademarks. In 1912 the annual sales of Edmonds tins passed the magic one million mark, and three years later annual sales were equivalent to six-and-a-half tins for every household in the country.

In 1908 Edmonds initiated further promotion for his powder with the publication of the first Sure to Rise *Cookery Book*. This contained 'economical everyday recipes and cooking hints', and was originally given away free to engaged couples. The Edmonds *Cookery Book* subsequently changed with the times, adapting to the widespread introduction of cooking by electricity from the 1920s and, later, metrication and the introduction of the microwave oven.

The sixty-ninth edition of the book appeared in 2017, and some of its 400 recipes acknowledged recent trends such as home-made pasta and gluten-free dietary requirements. And further to the baking powder that started it all, the Edmonds *Cookery Book* has become a national institution in its own right. Since 1908 it has sold some 4 million copies, qualifying it as the all-time bestselling New Zealand book.

It is a regular feature of classic examples of Kiwiana that their origins are often humble, often random. This was certainly the case with New Zealand's largest chain of grocery stores, Four Square, whose name and symbol both originated with a doodle.

The Four Square story began in the 1920s when the owners of small grocery stores in Auckland became concerned at the competition posed by the arrival of a new concept, the chain store, in particular those operating under the Self-Help banner. These began in Wellington in 1921 and enjoyed meteoric growth with stores reportedly springing up 'like mushrooms'.

To counter the growing threat of these chain stores, a group of Auckland grocers got together in 1922 and formed a co-operative, the first of several regional organisations that would eventually trade under the Foodstuffs name. Two years later, on 4 July 1924, the company secretary was on the telephone and while doodling on his desk calendar he drew lines around the date. This was the inspiration for the name of the company, Four Square. The fact that this had occurred on the 4th of July, American Independence Day, gave it additional relevance for a group of independent grocers.

A hand-painted glass sign of the new symbol, in red, gold and black, was provided for display in the window of each member store. Similar co-operatives were established in other regions throughout New Zealand, and existing stores were rebranded to trade under the new Four Square name. These businesses were linked for buying and advertising purposes but were individually owned and operated, so were not chain stores in the accepted sense of the term.

In addition to the familiar Four Square symbol,

in the early 1950s Foodstuffs was responsible for another well-known commercial image, that of the friendly grocer, Mr Four Square, now also referred to as 'Cheeky Charlie'. He first appeared in newspaper advertising and on posters, and was later to become an integral part of the company's national identity. Several real-life grocers have been suggested as the model for this symbolic grocer, among them George Allan, who operated several stores in Auckland.

Early in his career Mr Four Square appeared in different versions, but in 2007 he became standardised. He retained his cheeky smile, white apron and thumbs-up sign but lost the pencil behind his ear, while his facial makeover included a contemporary hairstyle, replacing his side-parting. In addition, in 1982 he had made the transition from advertising to fine art, when he was honoured by being included in a painting by Auckland artist Dick Frizzell.

In 1937 Foodstuffs launched another well-known name, the Pam's label (the possessive apostrophe was later dropped). Despite several theories as to who 'Pam' may have been – if in fact she had ever existed – the origin of the name is uncertain. Nevertheless, 'she' was first associated with tins of baking and custard powder, and Pams would go on to become the biggest grocery brand in New Zealand.

As at mid-2017 the Foodstuffs empire included 137 New World supermarkets and 56 PAK'nSAVE discount food warehouses around the country. The grocery business has become increasingly competitive, but years after that Independence Day doodle there are still 260 Four Square stores in existence, mostly to be found in the small towns of New Zealand.

Mr Four Square.

A NEW ZEALAND DAIRY FARM

R.C.H.5. Issued by the EMPIRE MARKETING BOARD.

Printed for H.M Stationery Office by St Michael's Press Ltd, West Norwood. S.E.27.

Down on the Farm

Gumboots and the smell of silage in the morning …

For the greater part of the time since European settlement, farming has played the major role in the nation's economy. Only tourism, and that only in recent years, has come close to matching the export receipts that agriculture provides. Agriculture is the wellspring not only of our economy but also of the Kiwi's practical nature.

Despite ever-increasing urbanisation there are still a lot of small agricultural-industry service towns in New Zealand and the pull of the land remains strong for many people. That this is so was shown by the wide following for the late lamented John Clarke's alter ego Fred Dagg and his Trevors, and for the equally missed Murray Ball and his creation of the cartoon rurality that is *Footrot Flats*. Both these reflected, and gave credence to, our feelings for the land, and to what has been described as 'cowpat patriotism'.

One of the most frequently quoted facts about New Zealanders is how they are outnumbered by their sheep. In the early 1980s, when the nation's sheep population reached an all-time high of 70.3

'Dog' is the hero of Footrot Flats, *a cartoon strip following the realities and fantasies of rural life and a dog struggling to make sense of it all.*

million this was certainly the case, with some 22 animals for every person. But since then sheep numbers have dropped dramatically to an estimated 27.34 million (at 30 June 2017), and there are now only six for every New Zealander. Nevertheless, sheep remain a feature of the national landscape, and continue to make an important contribution to the economy.

New Zealand was first introduced to sheep in 1793 by Captain Cook, who liberated a ram and a ewe in the Marlborough Sounds. But the pair did

not take to their new home, and the first successful establishment of a flock in this country took place on Mana Island, near Wellington, in 1834.

In order to provide suitable pastures for sheep, New Zealand's early farmers needed to remove the existing ground cover. Thick bush was destroyed by massive burn-offs, and the cleared land could then be ploughed, sown with grass and white clover and fenced into paddocks. Sheep could also assist in this conversion of the landscape; in 1844 farmers were advised that if broken land was sown with turnips, sheep would eat the turnips and, in the process, trample the undergrowth.

Merinos dominated New Zealand's early flocks, and provided its first export of wool. In fact, wool would become the longest sustained export commodity in this country's history. But because the Merino was found unsuitable for producing meat, New Zealand farmers began cross-breeding with other imported breeds to produce an animal with both a meatier carcass and the tougher fleece needed for the manufacture of woollens.

There was a turning point in national prosperity in 1882, when the first successful shipment of frozen meat from this country arrived in London. In addition to wool, New Zealand was now able to develop overseas markets for the edible parts of its sheep. This encouraged the development of sheep breeds which were not only better suited to New Zealand conditions, but also dual purpose, providing both meat and wool.

The country's agriculture now expanded rapidly, with the conversion of additional large swathes of bush into pastures for the growing population of sheep. Rural New Zealand became characterised by woolsheds – the distinctive buildings, typically sheathed in red-painted corrugated iron, where the annual shearing and the packing of fleeces into wool bales was carried out. There was a growing number of freezing works, where sheep and other animals ended their lives, and where few bodily parts were wasted.

Sheep farming was New Zealand's most important agricultural industry for over 130 years, from the 1850s to the late 1980s. Changes came in 1973 when Britain joined the European Union, then known as the European Economic Union or Common Market. New Zealand lost its traditional market, and needed to find alternatives. At home, the removal of subsidies previously enjoyed by farmers meant that sheep production now needed to be more mindful of market forces. As a result of a number of dramatic developments, the nation's sheep population went into a steady decline. At the same time, and in response to the new economic forces, farmers began to diversify into other areas such as forestry and viticulture, while dairying began to overtake sheep farming in terms of economic importance.

When it comes to dairying, a famous symbol on the country's export products has been the 'Anchor' trademark. This was derived from the anchor tattoo worn by one of the workers on the Waikato farm of Henry Reynolds, who first used this mark on his butter in 1886. Anchor continues today as one of the most highly regarded brands from Fonterra, New Zealand's largest company. Fonterra's approximate 30 per cent share of world dairy exports illustrates the high level of efficiency in our dairying practices and processes that has allowed New Zealand to carve out such a pre-eminent position while being so far from its markets.

This country's rural wardrobe is nothing else if not practical, from black bush singlets and Swanndris to gumboots.

With all the wool that was once produced, it's little wonder that a lot of it found its way into local clothing, such as the Swanndri. Created in 1937 by tailor John Kendrick, the Swanndri is the original rugged outdoor garment and was quickly adopted by bushmen and farmers. The original 'swanni', a dark green bush shirt, knee-length and single-coloured, was valued for the warmth it provided and protection

against showers – qualities derived from 100 per cent wool and a process that shrinks the woven cloth to increase its moisture-resistance. The original garment has spawned a range of work and leisure jackets and shirts that are exported around the world.

As for our gumboots, where would we be without them, as Fred Dagg sang. Ever since 1943 when its first rubber gumboot was made, Skellerup has set the standard for this type of footwear. And while other gumboots have come and gone, Skellerup's 'Red Band' boot has continued to be something of a New Zealand icon. This rugged and comfortable mid-calf gumboot first appeared in 1958, and its popularity hasn't been limited to the rural market. In this rainy and pleasant

LEFT *The 'swanni'.*
ABOVE *The classic 'Red Band' gumboot.*
OPPOSITE *Cowsheds, woolsheds, implement sheds – any kind of shed, not to mention dog kennels and water tanks – all the recipients of corrugated-iron treatment and creating what writer Geoff Chapple has described as an 'unremitting' ripple across the land.*

land it's also the perfect footwear for gardening and watching winter sports from the sideline. The New Zealand record for throwing a gumboot stands at 46.36 metres, set at Taihape's annual Gumboot Day where the phrase 'give it some welly' is given practical expression.

ABOVE *Variations on rural footwear at a stock yard sale.*
RIGHT *Cows are among a menagerie of corrugated-iron animals made by artist Jeff Thomson.*

Calf Day is a long-standing tradition at rural schools.

Keeping all of the country's cows and sheep inside their paddocks is the work of old reliable No. 8 fencing wire, and also the Taranaki gate. The home-made Taranaki gate is a good example of rural make-do. It is made of wire (either No. 8 or barbed), stapled to battens and strung between two strainer posts to which it is attached with loops of wire. The gate's value lies not only in its cheapness and the ability to be made on-site using to-hand materials and tools, but also because it can be adapted to sloping land and to wide and narrow gateways. Such improvised gates tend to be referred to as Taranaki gates wherever they're seen. Other 'Taranaki' prefixed expressions, such as Taranaki sunshine, meaning rain or drizzle, and Taranaki topdressing, which refers to cow manure lying in its naturally deposited state, are thought to reflect the tough times experienced by Taranaki farmers in the 1920s and 1930s.

Good Sports

When the obligatory weekend chores of home-improvement and lawnmowing have been disposed of, New Zealanders turn to their real interests, which for many Kiwis involve sport.

Rugby is of course still the main event. From school teams through clubs and regional sides to the All Blacks who continue to rule international rugby, despite some of the opposition occasionally closing the gap. When New Zealand's representative team first went to Britain in 1905 they lost just one game out of 35 played over the entire tour. It was during this tour that the team, known as 'The Originals', became the 'All Blacks'.

Your average All Blacks at the middle of the twentieth century were amateur players, fitting their rugby around their jobs (most likely as a farmer: many hailing from the backblocks of the King Country, the Wairarapa or North Canterbury – players such as Brian Lochore, the Meads brothers and Don Clarke). Despite the move to professionalism in the 1990s the game today continues to be as strong as ever at its regional grassroots. Nor has professionalism dented

the All Blacks' standing that includes a 77 per cent winning record in test matches, as well as being the only international side to have a winning record against every opponent.

While it may seem to be all about rugby, there is a plethora of other sporting activities that see hundreds of thousands of Kiwis taking to netball, hockey, bowls, yachting, athletics, rowing and cycling among other sports.

Running is another sport Kiwis have always been good at, particularly middle-distance races. In New Zealand, recognition for putting the country on its feet goes to one man – Arthur Lydiard, who enjoyed great success in coaching middle-distance runners in the 1960s to Olympic medals, among them Peter Snell, Murray Halberg and Barry Magee. Lydiard's training system emphasised strength

and stamina and carried Kiwi track athletes to international dominance for the next 20 years. The country's first jogging club was formed in 1962, and within a few short years the exploits of our golden runners had inspired tens of thousands of less extraordinary Kiwis to don running shoes and take to the parks and footpaths.

Then there's cricket. While rugby will thrash itself into a lather at the faintest whiff of defeat, with cricket it's the reverse: a couple of draws in a row or

ABOVE *The game continues to be as strong as ever at its regional grassroots.*
OPPOSITE *Legendary miler Peter Snell. The success of Arthur Lydiard's band of runners, Snell especially, was inspiring. Growing up at the time, if you couldn't or didn't want to be an All Black, well, there was always the possibility, it seemed, you might run a four-minute mile.*

Boundary 6.

Boundary 4.

Out.

ABOVE *Church cricket: an expressive man of the cloth might move a match along at a good clip while a more restrained one could put the getting of a result in doubt.*
RIGHT *Marching's origins go back to 'cheer-up' rallies during the Great Depression.*

the odd win and suddenly it's all on for the World Cup. If nothing else, however, cricket does provide a spot of philosophy. For while you may face the occasional bouncer or risk being caught out in the deep, each new delivery, like each new day, provides a chance to play on. It probably makes losing more bearable. In years gone by, pupils at Christ's College in Christchurch employed the rules of cricket in order to alleviate the tedium of chapel services. Each boy represented a team for the duration of a 10-wicket two-innings match, scoring on the basis of the hand movements from the minister unwittingly playing the role of umpire.

Messing about in small boats is second nature to a lot of Kiwis, starting when they're knee-high and

Making do: a rural paddock commandeered for a cricket match. The pitch does not appear to have been mown, or rolled, for the occasion. The match has attracted the attention of passing traffic, although not that of a grazing cow.

more often than not by way of a P-class or Optimist yacht. The legendary P-class was designed by Harry Highet who launched his prototype on New Year's Day in 1920 at Whangarei. It would be hard to find a top-class New Zealand yachtie who hasn't sailed one, and the P-class has been formative in New Zealanders winning at world yachting championships, not to mention the America's Cup.

And one mustn't forget marching. The discipline! The precision! *Eyes right!* Nearly 90 years after its emergence on the national scene, marching – part performance art, part sport – continues to have

a special place in the culture. Dating back to the Depression of the 1930s – the Auckland YWCA fielded a team in 1931 which gave 'cheer-up' rallies and demonstrations at charity events – marching is a uniquely New Zealand phenomenon despite elements being borrowed from American drum majorettes. Its heyday was in the 1950s when hundreds of teams of Midgets, Juniors and Seniors were going through their drills on sports fields and competing in national competitions that emphasised team discipline and appearance. Today, while fewer in number, its adherents are just as passionate.

On a rubber band and a prayer.

A non-sport sport, which New Zealand has made its own, is bungy jumping. Inspired by the 'land-diving' Pentecost islanders of Vanuatu, members of the Oxford University Dangerous Sports Club replaced the land-diving vines tied around the ankles with rubber bands. New Zealand technical and systems development brought the idea into the mainstream and international popularity. A jump from San Francisco's Golden Gate Bridge by the Oxford Dangerous Sports Club was the inspiration for New Zealanders AJ Hackett and Henry van Asch, who would develop the elastic cord ropes and the jumping itself into a perfect system that allowed anyone, young or old, to safely plunge headlong from great heights towards the rocks below. Hackett's own jumps are legendary – including leaps from helicopters and hot air balloons – with his 1987 bungy from the Eiffel Tower giving a global launch to his company's operations. Today bungy jumping at New Zealand sites attracts tens of thousands of visitors to this country each year.

An unidentified women's rugby team of the 1930s.

Summertime

The end of the calendar year in New Zealand meets the conclusion of the school and work year, adding extra frisson to Christmas preparations and summer holiday planning. After the forced march of a December trying to prepare for all of that, the country traditionally ground to a halt from Christmas through to the end of January as we all fled to the beach.

Given that the furthest you can ever be from the sea in New Zealand is something like 130 kilometres (it is the residents of Garston in Southland who must travel furthest for a dip in the sea), and as the great majority of us live little more than 10 kilometres from the coast, it's only natural that the seaside assumes such a large role in our lives. There are thousands of kilometres of coastline available, providing a rich profusion of bays and excellent beaches. From our suburban homes we head east and west to settle along the coast like so many migratory birds, making temporary homes in tents, caravans and baches. For a society already greatly egalitarian, the beach is a further levelling where labourers and business managers, farming folk and townies, the rich and the not-so-rich, blend together in a wonderful confusion of jandals, shorts and t-shirts, togs and hats: towelling, straw and baseball caps.

Once the motor car had opened up otherwise inaccessible parts of the coast to holiday-makers, Kiwis were able to build and enjoy that little slice of heaven called the bach (after 'bachelor'). The history of the bach is a rich tale of recycling and building in peculiar places. Many of the first baches were built from wood cast-offs, such as used car cases made from durable hardwoods like cedar. Old trams have also been put to good use, as has the occasional cave. Classic construction materials included fibrolite and board-and-batten and, of course, corrugated iron.

Right up until the 1980s the humble bach continued to mushroom along the country's coastline. In the years since, however, the growing appeal of coastal living has seen the bach become a luxury, now increasingly unaffordable to the average Kiwi. At the same time, what was once a spartanish bolthole has been increasingly replaced by proper houses replete with the kinds of mod-cons we were previously happy to leave behind. Some baches may

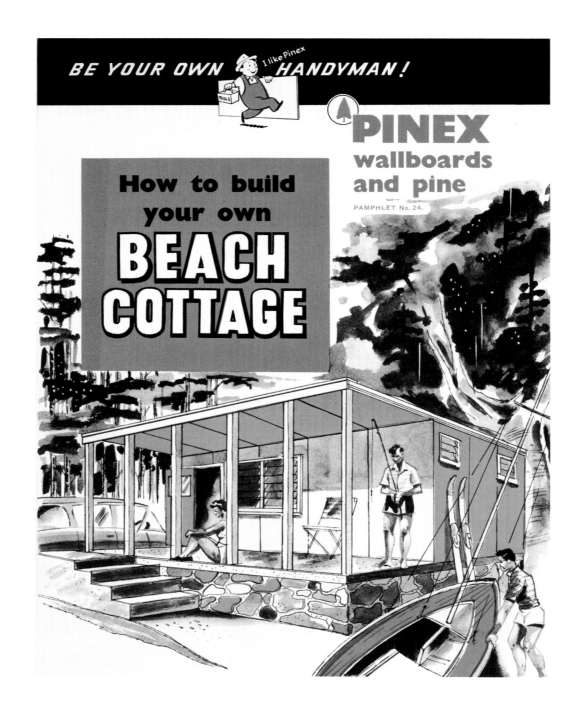

BE YOUR OWN HANDYMAN!

I like Pinex

PINEX
wallboards
and pine

PAMPHLET No. 24.

How to build
your own
BEACH
COTTAGE

uniquely as Jandals, a registered trademark name but one that like so many others has passed into common usage. The rubber Jandal (a contraction of 'Japanese sandal') was developed by New Zealand businessman Maurice Yock, who patented 'Jandal' in 1957. That first jandal was initially brown and white. Other colours eventually followed with blue proving the most popular.

Going on holiday before we all had cars was mostly a case of travelling by bus, train or ferry, as operated by New Zealand Railways and Road Services. Railways' steel roads could take you just about anywhere. Train travel in particular has contributed a fair amount of material to our national folk history, spawning customs, songs and artefacts. The refreshment-stop scrambles were once a well-known part of travelling the main trunk lines of both islands. These brief stops were part of the inconvenience, discomfort and, at times, adventure that was long-distance rail travel. On the North Island's 'Night Limited' service, stops

have bordered on the primitive but that was the point – and their charm.

The bach's original philosophy was simplicity, an eagerly anticipated contrast to the usual rules at home. The deadly metronome of working life was abandoned for the time being, replaced by holiday time. Meals were fairly informal and nobody got into too much trouble for bringing sand inside. There seemed little point in going to the effort of duplicating the cares of overly house-proud city domesticity at the beach, and so the bach became a handy retirement home for furniture and fittings that were past their best but still had years of life left in them.

Being on holiday also meant going barefoot or, at the most, donning the kind of footwear known elsewhere as thongs or flip-flops but in New Zealand

OPPOSITE *A home handyman project from summers past. This pamphlet contained everything you needed to know to build your own beach cottage. This was one of the more demanding of the projects offered by NZ Forest Products; one could choose to begin with the 'Pinex TV trolley'.*

It's the NIGHT LIMITED...

... premier express train on the Auckland-Wellington overnight service

SOUTHBOUND
Leaves Auckland 7.15 p.m., Sunday to Friday.
Arrives Wellington 9.30 a.m., Monday to Saturday.

NORTHBOUND
Leaves Wellington 7.15 p.m., Sunday to Friday.
Arrives Auckland 9.15 a.m., Monday to Saturday.

★ Sleeping-Car Service, including light supper and morning tea served to passengers in their cosy, private, two-berth cabins. £5/18/6 single; £11/6/- return.

★ Pressure-ventilated first-class coaches with individually adjustable reclining seats and ample leg room. £4/8/6 single; £8/6/- return.

★ Second-class coaches with comfortable foam-rubber seating for really low-cost travel. Only £3/1/- single; £5/12/- return.

OTHER EXPRESS TRAINS between Auckland and Wellington, with similar accommodation, leave Auckland at 3.30 p.m., Monday to Saturday, and 6 p.m. Sunday, and leave Wellington at 3.30 p.m., daily, including Sunday.

FOR TRAVEL COMFORT

The New Zealand Railways cup – virtually indestructible.

at Taihape, Frankton, Taumarunui and Palmerston North were places where you came to briefly for sustenance before falling back into your seat and onto your hire pillow for further fitful sleep.

As the train slowed into the platform there was a mad rush to get off to purchase a pie or sandwich and the obligatory cuppa. The tea and coffee, already milked, were poured from giant-sized metal teapots and everything was carried back on board. Mostly the refreshment stops were only long enough to join the queue and obtain your order – the train didn't wait around and eating and drinking had to be done back on board. If the food was unremarkable – although, really, at some ungodly hour of the morning a plain ham sandwich or pie took on five-star quality – at least the Railways crockery was distinguished, most memorably the famous Railways cup. Made by the

SERVICE

THE RAILWAY DEPARTMENT'S REFRESHMENT BRANCH GIVES TO ALL
PASSENGERS A FULL MEASURE OF SERVICE WITH HIGH-CLASS MEALS
AND REFRESHMENTS WHICH WILL SATISFY THE MOST FASTIDIOUS.

THE PLEASURE OF A SELECTION OF AN APPETISING BREAKFAST IS
AVAILABLE IN THE FOLLOWING MENU IN THE WELLINGTON
RESTAURANT ON ARRIVAL THIS MORNING. THE PRICE IS 2/- FOR
ADULTS, AND 1/- FOR CHILDREN UNDER 12 YEARS OF AGE.

MENU

FRUIT.
ROLLED OATS.
FISH:
SMOKED.   FRIED.
EGGS:
SCRAMBLED.   POACHED.   BOILED.
EGGS and BACON.
LAMB'S FRY· and BACON.
OMELETTES:
PLAIN.   SWEET.   SAVOURY.
GRILLS:
RUMP STEAK.   KIDNEYS.   CHOPS.
PORK SAUSAGES.

TEA.   COFFEE.   COCOA.

Enjoy Breakfast
in the
Railway Restaurant
WELLINGTON
STATION.

20,000 '11/38 - 14733

Hearty breakfast fare from New Zealand Railways.

Amalgamated Brick and Tile Company of Auckland, which became Crown Lynn Potteries in 1948, the company had been established to manufacture sewer pipes and electrical porcelains. During the Second World War the company diversified into making crockery for the US Navy stationed in New Zealand and in 1943 the company received its first order for crockery from New Zealand Railways. The new cups proved virtually indestructible, which they needed to be given the way that, some time later in the journey, they were rattled into wire baskets or boxes by guards working their way through the carriages.

Legendary among the refreshment stops was the one at Taumarunui, whose canteen was immortalised in song. 'Taumarunui on the Main Trunk Line' tells the story of a passenger on the Night Limited express train who falls in love with a woman running the canteen and decides to get a job as a fireman on the train in order to see her. Alas, his 'sheila' switches to the day shift. The Taumarunui stop closed in 1975 when the station's canteen sold its last sandwich and cup of tea. A decade or so later Crown Lynn also closed its doors, succumbing to the increasing flood of imported crockery lines.

Being at the seaside brought with it a diversity in the holidaymakers' diet, taking advantage of the free food that was at their doorsteps – fish, mussels, crayfish, tuatua, pāua and more. If the country's most distinctive bird is the kiwi, the marine equivalent is probably the pāua, a large and oval-shaped edible mollusc. It is known in the United States and Australia as abalone, but only the New Zealand pāua has a colourful inner shell, distinguished by iridescent blues, greens, pinks and purples.

Prized as a delicacy and for its decorative potential, the pāua has played an important part in the Māori world. The shell was used for infilling eyes in carved representations of ancestors, and also for fishing. Hooks, made of wood, shell and bone, also incorporated pāua, which flashed when moving

Pāua galore: the famous pāua-decorated living room of Myrtle and Fred Flutey.

through the water and attracted surface-feeding fish such as kahawai and barracouta.

There are three species of pāua found in New Zealand waters. The most familiar is the great or blackfoot pāua, while there is also the silver or yellowfoot and the virgin pāua. Another distinguishing feature of the pāua is the row of respiratory pores – breathing holes – along the side of the shell. It also has a muscular foot with strong suction power that enables it to cling tightly to rocky surfaces. A blunt instrument is needed to prise the animal from its natural habitat.

Pāua are found around the sub-tidal coastline of New Zealand. They prefer the colder waters of the southern parts of the South Island, where they grow larger and in greater numbers. The pāua's spectacular colours are the result of its diet of algae and seaweed. In 1901 Frederick W Hutton, director of the

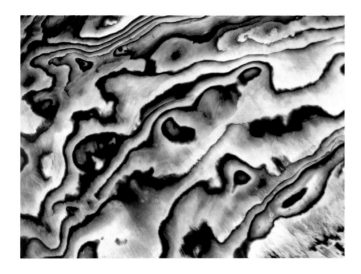

Canterbury Museum in Christchurch, explained that its iridescence was due to the shell being covered with large numbers of minute light-reflecting grooves.

Unsurprisingly, the decorative potential of pāua shell was quickly recognised. A growing souvenir industry arose, producing a wide range of items made from pāua shell, as well as kauri gum, greenstone and native woods. Pāua was used to embellish a number of domestic items too, from serviette rings to picture frames and book ends. (The pāua shell has also suffered the ultimate indignity of being used as an ashtray.)

In its natural state the edible part of the pāua is rubbery, so needs to be tenderised. This can be achieved either by hammering or, less violently, mincing. A batter is then applied, and after frying

One of the best known and most evocative depictions of the pōhutukawa was by Swedish-born artist Edward Fristrom. His Pohutukawa, *painted around 1905, shows a typical summer scene in New Zealand's North Island.*

each side for about a minute-and-a-half, the golden brown pāua fritters are ready to be served, perhaps with a squeeze of lemon.

One of the most remarkable chapters in the story of pāua is the collection made by Fred and Myrtle Flutey of Bluff, at the bottom of the South Island. Over a period of some 50 years the couple accumulated and decorated the walls of their living room with in excess of a thousand shells. The Pāua Shell House, as it became known, was a local landmark and destination for both national and international visitors. Following the deaths of Fred and Myrtle in the early 2000s, their now famous pāua shell collection was obtained by the Canterbury Museum and went on display in a reconstruction of their Bluff house.

Along with the sand and surf, a distinguishing feature of the coast in northern New Zealand is a tree, the pōhutukawa (*Metrosideros excelsa*). Its spectacular crimson flowers appear through December. One of New Zealand's most loved trees, the pōhutukawa

features in Māori legend. Tradition records that canoes bringing this country's earliest settlers, from east Polynesia, arrived at the time when the trees were in full bloom. Of particular significance to Māori is a gnarled pōhutukawa growing on the cliff at Cape Reinga, near the northern tip of New Zealand. This is said to be the place from where the spirits of the dead begin their journey back to their Pacific homeland, climbing down the roots of the tree to reach the underworld.

The pōhutukawa – along with rātā – is a member of the myrtle family and has hard, heavy and dark red heartwood. It is a hardy coastal evergreen, able to withstand wind and salt spray, and its aerial roots enable it to survive in the most difficult and inhospitable of environments. In fact, the pōhutukawa is the only tree capable of colonising bare lava. Distinguished by its twisted trunks and horizontally spreading branches, the tree grows up to 20 metres high and 35 metres wide, and can probably live a thousand years. A well-known pōhutukawa, believed to be the world's largest specimen (the tree has been introduced to parts of Australia and South Africa), grows at Te Araroa, some 174 kilometres from Gisborne on the North Island's East Coast. This giant is nearly 20 metres tall, has a spread of 38 metres, and is probably over 600 years old.

The pōhutukawa was much admired by early colonists from Britain; its timber was used for fencing, and in 1846 was recommended for ship construction and work for which curved timber was required. In 1853 a local poet wrote of the pōhutukawa's 'gorgeous flowers that outrival ours' – that is, English flowers – and around the same time pōhutukawa became known as the New Zealand Christmas tree, and was adopted as a substitute for the traditional holly and mistletoe.

The 1869 Christmas celebrations in the township of Thames, for example, included decorating the fronts of leading hotels with pōhutukawa, along with other floral arrangements. The growing appreciation of the tree was apparent in an Auckland newspaper article on the New Zealand forest, which referred to 'the luxuriant scarlet flowers that group in clusters over the crooked stems and broad branches of the magnificent pōhutukawa'.

Unfortunately, many pōhutukawa have become victims of the possum, which has developed a taste for the tree's leaves, buds, flowers and young shoots. In the late 1980s it was discovered that a large proportion of the country's stands of pōhutukawa, especially along the west coast of Northland, had been eliminated, or were at risk. This had been caused by forest clearance as well as possum browsing, and also choking from the matted roots of introduced weeds. In addition, the trees' roots, which evolved to spread over rocky ground, are exposed and are therefore vulnerable to damage by passing traffic and grazing stock. This drastic situation led to the establishment of Project Crimson, a charitable trust which aims to protect pōhutukawa and rātā by funding scientific research and community and school planting programmes.

Kiwis are great travellers and are joined over the summer months by an avian voyager, the bar-tailed godwit, one of a number of migratory wading birds that fly to and from New Zealand. The route the godwits use to travel northwards to their Alaskan breeding grounds

The pōhutukawa known as Te Waha O Rerekohu in the grounds of the Te Waha O Rerekohu Area School is thought to be the largest in the world.

ABOVE *The godwit is the master of migratory flight. Their migration south from their breeding grounds in Alaska to over-winter in New Zealand takes about eight days, during* *which the birds neither land, nor sleep.*
OPPOSITE *Playing with Opo, the legendary dolphin, in the mid-1950s, at Opononi in the Hokianga, Northland.*

is known as the East Asian–Australasian Flyway, a route that takes the birds across Indonesia, Japan and China over a period of six to seven weeks. This is done in stages with the birds spending time resting and feeding at stop-overs on the way.

Following the Northern Hemisphere summer spent at their breeding grounds, the godwits return to New Zealand when the weather starts to cool. The return leg south is an extraordinary non-stop flight over thousands of kilometres of Pacific Ocean; the longest of any non-seabird. After flying for more than a week the first of the godwits arrive back in late September, spending the summer at the tidal mudflats of a number of the country's harbours and estuaries, where they feed intensively to build up energy reserves before leaving again in March.

Afterword

In 1989 New Zealand's popular culture was given a name with the publication of our book *New Zealand! New Zealand! – In Praise of Kiwiana*. It was an idea which seemed to strike a chord; until then there hadn't really been a name for what seemed a grab-bag of cultural curiosities. An exhibition based on the book followed publication and 'Kiwiana' began to enter everyday speech.

It even achieved a legitimacy with its inclusion in *The New Zealand Dictionary* (1994), in which Kiwiana

was defined as 'any of many "collectibles", items redolent of New Zealand life and culture'. Further 'official' endorsement came the same year with the issue by New Zealand Post of the first of several series of Kiwiana postage stamps.

Today 'Kiwiana' turns up in company names, in the names of souvenir shops and backpacker hostels and is embodied in artworks and graphics. There is even a Kiwiana restaurant in New York City – the menu includes whitebait fritters, Anzac biscuits and pavlova. Despite the challenging and rapidly changing times it appears Kiwiana is in good heart.

Onward!

SB, RW

Acknowledgements

The authors acknowledge the assistance provided by a number of people and organisations for kindly making available information and materials for use in this book. In some cases the names of original sources have changed; the subsequent entity names are given in square brackets:

AJ Hackett Bungy NZ Ltd; Alexander Turnbull Library; Barry Young; Bluebird Foods [Edmonds]; Butland Industries [Goodman Fielder]; Cadbury Confectionery Ltd; Colin Edgerly; Dave Gunson; Debra Daley; Diogenes Designs Ltd; Foodstuffs (Auckland) Ltd [Foodstuffs North Island Ltd]; Foodstuffs New Zealand; Goodman Fielder NZ Ltd; J. Wattie Foods Ltd [Heinz Wattie's Ltd]; Jeff Thomson; Keith Lawson [Buzzy Bee Licensing Ltd]; Keith Money; Masport Ltd; Museum of New Zealand Te Papa Tongarewa; NZ Dairy Foods Ltd; NZ Rugby Museum; Nicholas Kiwi (Australia) [SC Johnson]; Oasis Industries [Coca-Cola Amatil NZ Ltd]; Phil Battley; Robin Ingram; Sanitarium Health Foods; Sara Lee Household & Body Care (NZ) Ltd; Swanndri Ltd; Tip-Top Ice Cream Co. Ltd; Underwood Engineering; Unilever NZ Ltd; US Geological Survey; J.H. Whittaker & Sons Ltd; Yates.

Illustration Credits

[S.C. Johnson] **36** Image ©Rod Morris www.rodmorris.co.nz **37** ATL 'Corner of Herbert and Manners Streets [Wellington].' Gordon Burt Collection - F-117864-1/2 **38** Geoffrey Short **39** Nicholas Kiwi (Australia) [S.C. Johnson] **40** ATL 'Lady Plunket.' S.P. Andrew Ltd: Portrait negatives. 1/1-014571-G **42** (upper) ATL 'Olympic Stationery Ltd: Birds of New Zealand; an Olympic production. School writing pad 9G. North Island kiwi, Apteryx mantelli. Series no. 6, Subject no. 46 [1950-1960s?].' Eph-B-Stationery-1960-01 **42** (lower) ATL 'Small patient at the Wellington Dental Clinic.' F-105154-1/2 National Publicity Studios Collection **43** Department of Education **44** ATL 'Primary school boys drinking their school milk, Linwood, Christchurch.' Pascoe, John Dobree, 1908–1972: Photographic albums, prints and negatives. 1/4-000033-F **46** The collection of Tip-Top Company Ltd **47** *Otago Daily Times* **50** Steven La Plante **51** (upper) Masport Ltd **51** (lower) Yates **52** (lower) Nitr/Shutterstock.com **54** Butland Industries Ltd [Goodman Fielder Ltd] **55** ATL 'For salads, for sandwiches, for cooking; no rind, no waste, does not dry. Manufactured by NZ Cheese Ltd. [1940-50s].' Eph-A-FOOD-1930s-03 **56** ATL 'Vincents Dairy, Paraparaumu Beach.' G-46589-1/2 **57** (lower) The collection of J. Wattie's Canneries Ltd [Heinz Wattie's Ltd] **59** (upper) ATL 'Soldiers eating sausage rolls, Selles, France.' Royal New Zealand Returned and Services' Association: New Zealand official negatives, World War 1914-1918. 1/2-012967-G **60** ATL 'Anna Pavlova.' 1/2-089575-F **61** Natasha Grigel/Shutterstock.com **62** (upper) Collection of Oasis Industries Ltd [Coca-Cola Amatil NZ Ltd] **62** (lower) ChameleonsEye/Shutterstock.com **63** (lower) The collection of Bluebird Foods Ltd [Edmonds Ltd] **65** Foodstuffs NZ **66** ATL 'Newbould, Frank, 1887–1951: A New Zealand dairy farm.' R.C.H.5. Issued by the Empire Marketing Board. Printed for H.M. Stationery Office by St Michael's Press Ltd, West Norwood, S.E. 27 [ca 1927]. Eph-D-TRADE-1927-01 **67** Diogenes Designs Ltd **68** patjo/Shutterstock.com **70** (lower) Swanndri NZ Ltd **71** Molly Marshall/Shutterstock.com **72** (upper) Geoff Mason **72** (lower) Jeff Thomson **73** ATL 'Unidentified members of an agricultural class with their calves.' G-13320

1/1 **74** Unknown **76** Grant Sheehan **77** *The New Zealand Herald* **78** (lower) *The New Zealand Herald*. 'The Remuera Guards (1960).' **79** ATL G-28810-1/2 **80** AJ Hackett Bungy NZ **81** ATL 'Unidentified women's rugby team. F-66915-1/2 **82** ATL 'Holidaymakers and cars on Maretai Beach, Manukau City.' Whites Aviation Ltd: Photographs. WA-59174-F [Part of WA-59174-FP] **84** ATL 'Be your own (I like Pinex) handyman. Pinex wallboards and line.' New Zealand Forest Products Ltd: Pamphlet no. 24 – How to build your own beach cottage [ca 1960] [Catalogues and price lists, ephemera advertising and listing building and home improvement supplies. 1960s] Eph-B-BUILDING-SUPPLIES-1960-01-24 **85** (upper) Paul Thompson **87** ATL 'The Railway Department's Refreshment Branch gives to all passengers a full measure of service with high-class meals … Menu. Enjoy breakfast in the Railway Restaurant, Wellington Station. 20,000/11/38 - 14733 [1938].' New Zealand Railways: Service. Eph-A-RAIL-1938-03 **88** Rob Suisted/naturespic.com **89** (lower) Auckland Art Gallery Toi o Tamaki. 'Pohutukawa.' Edward Fristrom oil on card, circa 1905, purchased 1967 **91** ATL 'Te Waha O Rerekohu, pohutukawa tree at Te Araroa.' Goodall, Gladys Mary, 1908– : Scenic photographs of New Zealand. GG-04-0102-1 **92** United States Geological Survey and Phil Battley **93** *The New Zealand Herald* **94** News Media (Auckland) Ltd.